A light broke in upon my soul—
It was the carol of a bird;
    It ceased—and then it came again,
The sweetest song ear ever heard.

ADAPTED FROM A POEM BY LORD BYRON

The Gift of Birds

Contents

Library of Congress CIP Data: page 173

Of Hollow Bones and Treetop Homes

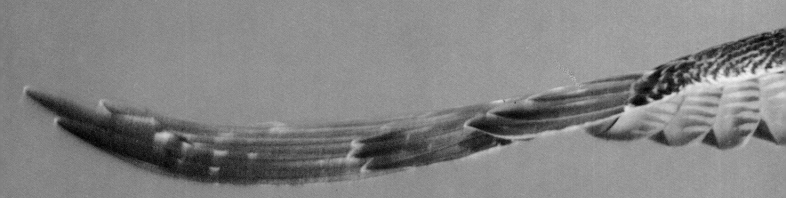

The Nature of Birds

F ine feathers will not alone make fine birds, Aesop tells us. I should think they would go a long way toward it, however, for it is feathers that make birds. All birds and no other creatures have them. The form ranges from the fluffy to the stiff (you can sleep in down or write with a quill) and from the nearly round and cupped to the nearly linear. But characteristically the feather is an oblong plane, a vane, given longitudinal rigidity by a median hollow shaft, extending almost to its end. To precisely the required degree it is elastic and flexible, especially toward its margins. So fine in structure as to be translucent and if not too heavily pigmented even almost transparent, it is also extremely strong for its weight. The muffled thunder of a grouse's whirring wings in the take-off expresses the force the frail-seeming sails sustain.

The vane is a web of fine ribs rooted to the shaft on either side and called barbs because they extend diagonally backward from the point of the feather, the end from which the shaft projects. The barbs are themselves very like feathers. Each consists of a central shaft fringed on either side with what might also be called barbs but are known as barbules. These bear microscopic hooks on one side and flanges on the other. The hooks of one barbule engage with the flanges on the adjacent barb, somewhat as the two sides of a zipper interlock. When the vane of a feather is rent a bird need only pass the two edges through its beak to rejoin the barbs, as a zipper opening is closed by running the slide up it. A large flight feather may have 500 barbs on either side of the shaft and as many barbules, on the average, on either side of each barb.

It is of course not feathers alone that make birds the flying machines they are. In almost every way the reptilian structure [birds evolved from reptiles—Ed.] has been radically redesigned for flight.

Toothed, bony jaws, being too heavy, especially so far out in front, have been replaced by a beak, light but strong, fastened to a skull pared to translucent thinness but strengthened by internal struts; such chewing as is necessary is done in the gizzard. The conventional vertebrate tail with its heavy links had to be dispensed with. The need has been to have both wings and legs join the body close to and above its center of gravity. So contrived, the bird will be neither front-heavy while walking nor rear-heavy while flying and not be top-heavy at any time. This has been achieved by foreshortening the body and affixing the wings and legs at its top.

Evolution has both suppressed parts of the higher vertebrate skeleton in birds and developed others to bear

Beaks are tools adapted to the type of food each bird species seeks. With its beak, the flamingo (1) strains minute plants and animals from water and mud, the woodpecker (2) chisels wood to reach insects, the kestrel (3) tears meat, the evening grosbeak (4) cracks seeds, and the bittern (5) grasps fish. The yellow-breasted chat (opposite) catches insects but also eats berries in autumn and winter.

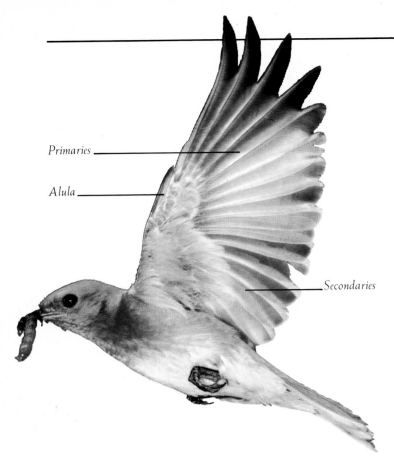

Primaries

Alula

Secondaries

The main flight feathers are the primaries and secondaries (above). During flight, the tightly locked barbs on each vane—magnified by a water droplet at right—allow very little air to slip through. The alula feathers increase lift during slow flight.

greater stresses. In both fore- and hind-limbs bones have been eliminated and fused. Wrists and ankles have been especially modified. The fourth and fifth fingers have disappeared. The second and third, reduced in parts and connected, make up the narrow "hand," into which the outer flight feathers are set—the primaries. (The next rank, the secondaries, are set in one of the two forearm bones.) One toe has been dropped in all birds, two in most ground-dwellers and three in the Ostrich, giving it the semblance of a cloven hoof. Development and fusion of shoulder bones has produced a strong pectoral saddle, into which the wings fit. Except in the neck, which is outstandingly flexible, the vertebrae have been compressed or fused together, up to 23 of them in the strong pelvic saddle containing the hip-joints. The pectoral assemblage, the compressed back vertebrae and the carapace-like pelvis form the top of a light, firm skeletal basket, of which the sides are the ribs (each with a lateral projection overlapping its neighbor behind) and the bottom is the breastbone. In the basket are the internal organs.

In flying birds the breastbone is deepened into a keel, to which the powerful wing-muscles are attached. Among the muscles that pull the wings down and bear the brunt of flight are, most surprisingly, those that raise them. These taper on the outer end to a tendon that passes between the shoulderblades and attaches to the upper side of the wing-bone so that the contraction of the muscle is equivalent to pulling down on a rope that passes

over a pulley: the object on the other end goes up. This ingenious contrivance, by which all wing muscles, which make up a substantial part of a flying bird's weight, are beneath the back, contributes to a low center of gravity and stability in flight.

Except in the smallest birds and in diving-birds, the larger bones are hollow. On the principle that a tube is stronger than a rod of the same amount of material, this gives strength with lightness. The bones bearing the primary feathers of large, soaring birds are reinforced by an internal trusslike system of struts that makes them worthy of exhibition as works of art.

An efficient engine keeps the avian apparatus operating at the high level of output required. The two-chambered reptilian heart has been enlarged to four, as in mammals, so that incoming blood may be completely relieved of its burden of waste products from combustion and be wholly charged anew with oxygen before being recirculated to the muscles and other organs. Birds have gone beyond mammals, however, in carrying the same principle over into breathing. In avian lungs air is pumped through a remarkable system of air sacs, five or more in number, that branch off the lungs to occupy much of a bird's body and, in large, soaring birds, extend even into the hollows of the major bones. In Frigate-birds and some of our Western grouse the neck sacs are visible and highly colored and are inflated in courtship display; the Spruce Grouse and Prairie Chicken expel the air from theirs to make a booming or moaning sound. Acting as bellows, the sacs supplement the lungs, which they greatly exceed in volume, and make possible the supply to the blood of the relatively huge amount of oxygen a bird requires. Bellows and lungs must work fast, moreover. A bird's respiration may reach 300 or 400 breaths a minute, or four or five times the rate while the bird is at rest; it is slower in the larger birds. To move the oxygen-bearing blood to the needy tissues a bird's heart is large, muscular and superpaced. Even during inactivity a chicken's heart-beat is 300 a minute, a small bird's twice that. The latter may increase to 1,000 or more when the system is taxed.

To fuel their engines at the tempo demanded of them, birds depend for the most part on energy-giving foods high in proteins—insects and other forms of animal life, seeds and nuts—or rich in sugars. Processing is swift: fruit given to young Cedar Waxwings, an investigator (M. M. Nice) found, was passed through the digestive system in 16 minutes. The amount consumed is also great, especially in a relative sense among small, active birds: hummingbirds have been known to take in daily twice their weight in nectar, the most directly energy-producing of all foods. With such stepped-up metabolism, there is the problem of temperature. Conversion of fuel to energy produces heat; even birds, adjusted as they are to internal temperatures that would kill us in short order, would burn up in flight without an exceptionally efficacious heat-dispersal system. This the air sacs provide. In cooling the blood they play as vital a role as in supplying it with oxygen.

A gull's skeleton (right) reveals adaptations for a life of flight: a strong, light framework achieved by slender, hollow bones (detail below); a toothless beak (1) instead of a heavy jaw; braced ribs with a fused "wishbone" (2) for wing support; hand and wrist bones (3) reduced in number and fused; and an enlarged breastbone with deep keel (4) for holding the muscles needed to power the wings.

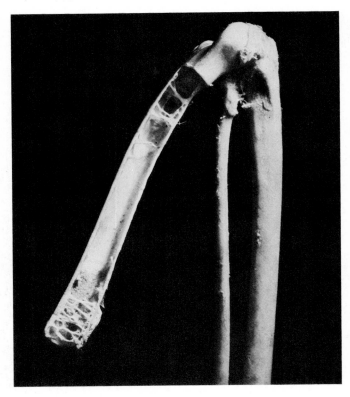

Two other properties are essential for successful flight, whether by living organisms or self-guiding missiles. There must be sensors capable of accurate, constant apprehension of what is ahead and a computer to receive the information and instantly instruct the guidance mechanism of needed changes in course. That birds are well endowed in both respects cannot be doubted by anyone who has seen them shoot swervingly through networks of branches or visualized nocturnal birds navigating and locating their prey in forests too dark to reveal the hand before the face to a human being. The hearing of birds by human standards is preternaturally acute. A Barn Owl with eyes sealed can zero in on a mouse by its faint rustling in the leaves and strike it. But undoubtedly it is the light-gathering power of their eyes that chiefly serves the navigational needs of nocturnal birds. Owls' eyes, which may be as large as a human being's, are ten times as efficient in this as ours.

There is no eye like a bird's eye. Change of focus in human vision depends on a muscle to contract and thicken the lens and on the natural resilience of the lens to restore it to its original shape. In birds there are muscles to do both jobs and others that change the shape of the cornea as well. They make possible an all-but-instantaneous shift in focus from sharp perception of objects at the limit of visibility to those a few beaks' lengths away. And a bird's perception is sharp indeed. Where the human eye has 200,000 visual cells per square

millimeter in the place of greatest concentration in the retina—the fovea—G. L. Wall in his study of the vertebrate eye reports that these reach as high as one million in the European Buzzard (the equivalent of our Red-tailed Hawk), which he believes gives it a visual acuity at least eight times ours.

Birds' eyeballs are so large that they nearly meet at the septum. Adding musculature to move them would mean a larger skull and increased weight, and it has been dispensed with. Birds' eyes are fixed. The handicap, as it would be for us, is overcome in the great majority of birds by the placement of the eyes well back on the sides of the head. Here they command a nearly full field of view. A bird has almost all its surroundings under observation simultaneously and continuously, half with one eye, half with the other. It is not readily taken by surprise. The price is that there is not much overlap of the fields of vision of the two eyes. The habit of birds of cocking their heads is the corollary of monocular vision; they can best get a fix on an object with the direct stare of a single eye. Owls are different. With forward-looking eyes and protruding corneas they have a complete overlap; everything they see, they see with both eyes. Because their field of vision is relatively narrow and their eyes immobile they are constantly swiveling their heads when on the alert; and they have the advantage of being able to look straight behind them. (All birds are compensated for their fixity of gaze by extreme suppleness of neck. Hawks stand midway between owls and other birds in the placement and scope of their eyes.)

An advantage of binocular, or stereoscopic vision, in movable eyes is in facilitating the gauging of distances; the eyes, working together, converge on close objects, the more so the closer, the less so the more distant. If you close one eye and reach out, quickly, to put a finger on a spot at arm's length you are apt to find that you miss it. In monocular vision distance must be judged by the diminution of the apparent size of an object with remoteness, by its position on an imaginary tape-measure laid out on the ground between the viewer and the horizon or by the difference between its apparent movement and that of other objects nearer and farther when the viewer, or at least his head, moves. An owl's abrupt, rather ludicrous shifts of head from side to side while its gaze remains fixed on a target may have the purpose of exploiting this principle.

If the messages streaming from a bird's retina into the optic nerve are comprehensive and clear, its brain is well designed to handle them. To receive and classify the rapid fire of images there are large optic nerves, indicating a capacity for visual association—we are told—comparable with man's. The cerebellum is also large and well developed: it provides for precisely ordered responses to incoming stimuli of all kinds, automatically, instantaneously, through reflex action. A bird need not stop to think. It needs only to see or hear and spontaneously beat its wings in the magnificent, feathered flight that distinguishes birds from all other forms of life.

Charlton Ogburn

Of Feather and Wing

Whated Leonardo da Vinci and later Otto Lilienthal and the French glider pioneers studied birds in order to learn the principles of flight, their concentration naturally was focused on the motions of wings and tail. But these movements turned out to be so fast, complex and subtle that their analysis was extremely difficult. Even today much remains to be learned of them.

One of the first facts revealed by the high-speed camera was that wings do not simply flap up and down. Nor do they row the bird ahead like oars. The actual motion is more that of sculling a boat or screwing it ahead by propeller action, a kind of figure-eight movement.

A bird's "hand" (outer wing) is longer than the rest of its "arm" (wing) but it has almost as complete control over it as a man has. It can twist its "hand" to any position, spread its ten primaries, waggle or twiddle them, shrug its shoulders, even clap its "hands" together behind its head and in front of its breast. That is why wing motion is so complex, variable, and hard to comprehend.

The powerful downstroke that obviously lifts and propels the bird also is a forward stroke, so much so that the wings often touch each other in front of the breast and almost always come close at take-off and climb. Many people have trouble understanding this fact proven by the camera until they reflect that it is likewise forward motion of the airplane wing that generates lift. Just as a sculling oar or a propeller drives a boat ahead by moving at right angles to the boat's motion, so does the force of the bird's wing resolve itself into a nearly perpendicular component.

Even the wing's upstroke plays its part in driving the bird upward and onward—for the same reason. This quick flip of recovery takes half the time of the downstroke and has much less power, but is still part of the sculling motion that is almost peristaltic—like a fish in the sea or a snake in the grass—probably closest of all to the rotor screw action of a moving helicopter: forward and down, backward and up and around.

The pliable feathers at the wing's tip and trailing edge bend according to the changing pressures, revealing how

In level flight, the raised wings are pulled downward and forward to create lift and thrust, and then upward and backward to complete their figure-eight motion. In landing, the wings control the speed of descent by changing shape to hold more or less air.

the air is moving. The downstroke plainly compresses them tightly upon each other the whole length of the outstretched wing, each feather grabbing its full hold of air, while the upstroke, lifting first the "wrist," then the half-folded wing, swivels the feathers apart like slats in a Venetian blind to let the air slip by. It is an automatic, selective process, the different movements overlapping and blending smoothly, the "wrists" half up before the wing tips stop descending, the "forearms" pressing down while the tips are yet rising. The convexity of the wing's upper surface and the concavity of its lower aid this alternate gripping and slipping of the air—this compression of sky into a buoyant cushion below the wing while an intermittent vacuum sucks from above—this consummate reciprocal flapping that pelicans accomplish twice a second, quail twenty times, and hummingbirds two hundred times!

Birds are clearly way ahead of the airplane in aileron or roll control; some, like ravens and roller pigeons, close their wings to make snap rolls just for fun or courting. And the same bird superiority holds in the case of flaps which brake the air to reduce speed in landing, the birds fanning out their tails for this purpose as well as their wings. Web-footed birds such as geese usually steer and brake with their feet also, and inflect their long necks like the bow paddle of a canoe to aid in steering and balancing.

The tail is of course intended primarily for steering—steering up and down as well as to right and left. Some birds with efficient tails can loop the loop, fly upside down, or do backward somersaults like the tumbler pigeon. Small-tailed birds such as ducks are handicapped by not being able to make any kind of sharp turns in the air, though their tails steer well enough in water and in slapping the waves on take-off from water. The male whidah bird has such a long tail that on a dewy morning he actually cannot get off the ground until the sun has evaporated the extra weight from his trailer. The variety of bird tails never ends, nor does the multiplicity of functions. Furled to a mere stick or fanned out 180° and

skewed to any angle, tails serve for everything from a stabilizing fin to a parachute, from a flag to a crutch.

Man cannot hope to match the bird in sensitivity of flying control, mainly because he usually has to think air or read it off instruments, while the bird just feels air everywhere on his feathers and skin. This is not to say, however, that the bird is a faultless flyer. Birds make plenty of mistakes—even forced landings! Not a few are killed in crashes. Usually bird slip-ups happen so fast they go unnoticed. But when you get a chance to watch a flight of birds coming in to land in slow-motion movies you can see them correcting their errors by last-moment flips of tail or by dragging a foot like a boy on a sled. If a landing bird discovers he lowered his "flaps" too soon he still can ease off these air brakes by raising his wings so that his secondaries spill wind, his primary feathers remaining in position for lateral or aileron control. But lots of times excited birds do not notice their mistakes soon enough and lose flying speed while trying to climb too steeply, or fall into a spin from tight turns or from simply misjudging the wind. Once they have ceased making headway they tumble downward just as surely as a stalled airplane.

I saw a heron one day muff a landing in a tree, stall, and fall to the ground, breaking his leg. This is particularly apt to happen to heavy birds like ducks when they are tired. Sometimes ducks lose half a pound on a long migratory flight and are so exhausted on letting down that they splash into the water and cannot take off again for hours.

The energy required of a heavy bird at take-off of course is very great. It has been estimated at five times normal cruising energy. Many birds, like the swan, need a runway in addition to the most furious beating of wings to get up enough speed to leave the ground. Others like the coot are lighter but low-powered and take off like a 1915 scout plane missing on three cylinders. All birds naturally take off against the wind for the same reason that an airplane does: to gain air speed, which is obviously

The young albatross below, wings oddly angled to catch the wind, is learning what pelicans and swans (bottom and opposite) confirm by their abrupt hops and graceful strides: birds must exceed a certain speed to become airborne. Landing can become a comic scene of arched wings and dragging feet, as the pelican at right reveals.

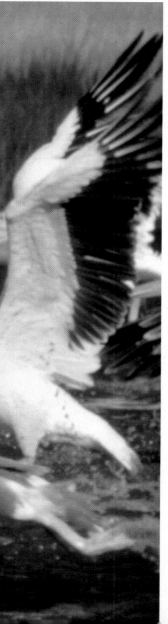

more significant than ground speed at take-off. You have surely noticed that birds feeding by the lee roadside will often take off across the path of an approaching car, actually tempting death to gain the wind's help.

Heavy birds that dwell on cliffs of course have the advantage of being able to make a catapult take-off, dropping into a steep glide until they build up flying speed—but again they must beware of landing at a place where this needed gravitational asset is not available. The penalty for lack of such foresight can well be death.

I heard of a loon that made the mistake of alighting on a small pond set amid a forest of tall pines. When he wanted to take off an hour later he found himself stymied. He could not climb steeply enough to clear the trees or turn sharply enough to spiral out. He was seen thrashing along over the water, whipping the waves with his wings to get under way, even pedaling at the water desperately with his webbed feet before getting into the air. He almost made it a couple of times but also nearly got killed crashing into the big trees, then plowing back through the underbrush on his sprained wishbone. Finally he had to give up. But this particular loon was lucky. After four frustrated days in his pond jail a very strong wind came up and enabled him to take off and climb so steeply against it that he just brushed between the tree-tops and was free!

A very different and special capacity is required in bird formation flight or mass maneuvering. Sand-pipers, plover, turnstones, sanderlings, and other small shore birds are all expert in this sort of flying, which seems to depend on extreme quickness of eye and a speed of selfless response not equaled elsewhere in nature. No one knows exactly how this amazing unity of action is accomplished or why.

When birds migrate they often fly in V formation and for the same reason that the Air Force does. It is the simplest way to follow a leader in the sky while keeping out of his wash and retaining good vision. Birds instinctively do it, peeling off from one heading to another and sometimes chasing after man-made gliders. They even have been seen pursuing power planes until they were unable to keep up with them.

Lots of birds, far from feeling jealous of human trespassing in their ancient territory, seem to get such a kick out of airplanes that they hang around airports just like human kids watching the big ones take off and land. Many a time I've seen sea gulls at the big Travis Air Base near San Francisco flapping nonchalantly among the huge ten-engined B-36 bombers while their motors were being run up. The smoke whipping from the jets in four straight lines past the tail accompanied by that soul-shaking roar would have been enough to stampede a herd of elephants but the sea gulls often flew right into that tornado for fun. When the full blast struck them they would simply disappear, only to turn up a few seconds later a quarter mile downwind, apparently having enjoyed the experience as much as a boy running through a hose—even coming around eager-eyed for more.

Guy Murchie

The Mysterious Magic of Birdsong

There is no sound more welcome than the song of birds. This is not only because of its varied beauties but for a deeper reason. Birdsong is a language—one without words, but with a meaning. We cannot fully understand it, but one thing within the mystery of birdsong we can be sure of. Its magic comes bubbling out of the deepest sources of springtime well-being. It is a yea-saying to life and its challenges.

For the *why* of bird singing, science has a few answers—none of them complete. One of the most precisely assured is that a bird sings in order to stake out a claim to his bailiwick for nesting. The migrating males, arrriving first in the springtime, proclaim each a certain territory as his own.

In some sunny, reedy swamp you may have heard the chorus of the red-winged blackbirds loud in song before ever the streaked females appear on the scene. "Konkeree!" they whistle, and it might be translated, at that moment, as "Here I am! Here I stay! This is mine—this patch of reed and sun and water."

As the females come winging from the south, the males sing to win themselves a mate. It is hard to doubt that the females are attracted by the virtuosos among them. And, having won his lady, the male sings through the nesting season, perhaps to please her, certainly because he is so full of the vernal surge of life that it just naturally bursts out in birdsong. This is proved by the fact that a solitary captive, unable to win a place to call his own or to draw to himself a mate, will in the springtime sing on in his prison, day after day. The spring is within him, and that is reason enough for song.

With the hatching of the nestling, song lessens. As breadwinner and grub gatherer, the father bird has less time for operatics. Certain species may rear a second brood and thus renew their musical efforts into midsummer. But this song lacks the fullness of the spring singing season; indeed it is sometimes sung almost with closed bill, so that only the nearby listener can catch it.

The time of day, as well as the time of year, influences birdsong. The coming of light seems to prompt singing in most of our familiar winged neighbors. But, if you listen to a dawn chorus, you will note that each kind of bird sings at his chosen moment. Again toward late afternoon there is an impetus to song, softer than the daybreak music. And certain birds, like the vesper sparrow, are drawn to sing with the coming of dusk. Others, like the whippoorwill, are vocal only at night. Still others, most famed of them the nightingale, sing both by day and by dark.

The marvelous spontaneity of fine birdsong is a mystery. Was the wild torrent from the canyon wren's throat once packed away, an inherited gift, in the egg from which he broke? Did the brown thrasher come by his lovely melodies the same way? Ornithologists give us a paradoxical answer. It has been concluded that, generally speaking, the simple call notes of a bird are born in him when he is hatched, but that true song may be partly inherited and partly learned, or entirely learned.

A group of English researchers under W. H. Thorpe at Cambridge University, for example, have found that when a young chaffinch is taken from the nest and reared alone, it sings but a poor and restricted version of the song of its kind in the wild. This, they suggest, may be taken as the basic inherited song pattern. But give the little prisoner in solitary confinement a fellow chaffinch, and his song improves as he listens to his companion. Song, in short, stimulates song. And who doubts it on a fine May morning when the bird chorus is in full swing?

Some birds incorporate in their singing the songs of other species. The catbird, the jay and the mockingbird have a reputation for imitation, though the song of the latter—which has been reported as having 32 imitations within it—may be varied less by mimicry than by sheer native virtuosity. An old gentleman we knew raised blue jays in cages in his office, to see what they could be taught. His prize pupil was one that imitated perfectly not only the squeak of his office chair and the family whistle for the dog, but also the sound of the children knocking at the door and calling to be let in.

Whatever the bird voices that stir you, they are likely to be those you heard early in life, for it is the birdsong of home that has the most meaning for all of us. For many, indeed, there are passages in life scored for accompanying birdsong. For us a shared growing-up in Illinois was full of the rollicking lays of the bobolink, of the contented lament of mourning doves, of the tinkling notes of the goldfinch on his undulant flight—one of the few birds that sing on the wing. Through the years, in many places, runs a musical thread on which dear memories are strung.

There is the ultimate mystery of birdsong—not just the incomprehensible communication between one feathered singer and others of his kind, but the wordless and magical meaning brought to the wondering human senses by a wild, sudden beauty that lifts the heart.

— **Donald and Louise Peattie**

A red-winged blackbird, vocal harbinger of spring in some parts of the U.S., attracts up to six mates with his gurgling "Konkeree!"

How Red the Tooth and Claw?

The discovery that birds claim and defend territories is often thought of as a twentieth-century achievement because that behavior has only been understood in detail since H. Eliot Howard published his *Territory in Bird Life* in 1920. Actually, Aristotle made some observations on bird economics. In *Historia Animalium* he wrote, "The fact is that a pair of eagles demands an extensive space for its maintenance, and consequently cannot allow other birds to quarter themselves in close neighborhood." In the third century B. C., Zenodotus wrote, "One bush does not shelter two robins." Also of robins Konrad von Gesner said in 1555, "*Erithacus avis est solitaria*," and G. P. Olina in 1622, "It has a peculiarity that it cannot abide a companion in the place where it lives and will attack with all its strength any who dispute this claim." Buffon wrote in the eighteenth century that nightingales "are also very solitary . . . they select certain tracts, and

oppose the encroachments of others in their territory. But this conduct is not occasioned by rivalship, as some have supposed; it is suggested by solicitude for the maintenance of their young, and regulated by the extent of ground necessary to afford sufficient food." Gilbert White thought that sexual rivalry was behind the formation of territories, writing that "it is to this spirit of jealousy that I chiefly attribute the equal dispersion of birds in the spring over the face of the country." We know now that the territories are defended because they are the homesites where family life is carried on, and that the limits are often defined by the food requirements. Most of the songbirds, whose young will be hatched in outside nests, need enough feeding space near the nest so that the tiny offspring will never be left very long by their parents. The nestlings must have comparatively enormous quantities of nourishment, very fre-

quently, or their energy drops, they become chilled, then cease to accept the food that is brought to them, and soon die. Birds that nest in holes in trees are less exposed and keep warmer, and therefore the parents can forage farther afield. The territory of those parents may be only the tree itself.

If a bird is returning to last year's nesting site, he knows exactly what shape and size he wants his territory to be, and he doesn't waste even an hour before taking up his position on various points on his borders, singing to announce that he is the owner of all the land enclosed by these stations. In the case of most birds it is more than one tree but not often more than an acre. If he is a new, young bird, it may take two days, rarely longer, to look over the ground and decide how much space he will defend. Meanwhile his neighbors are deciding what *they* will defend, and dis-

agreements are settled by the birds singing at each other. Beautiful as the bird songs are, some of them, too, are arguments, and it speaks well for the birds that controversies almost always are settled without physical combat.

A robin will value a nice stretch of lawn which promises a good harvest of worms; finches will want crops of seeds; warblers and swallows an abundance of insects. These special needs have a bearing on the kind of territory a bird will try to establish, of course. Suppose a bird makes a miscalculation? There is a fine tree for a nest in the area that the robin selects, but the lawn below may

The size of a bird's territory depends largely on its food habits and the abundance of its species. A whooping crane's territory (left) ranges from 400 to 640 acres. Flamingos (above) live in dense colonies, where nests may lie within two feet of each other.

21

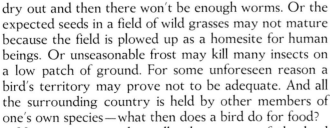

dry out and then there won't be enough worms. Or the expected seeds in a field of wild grasses may not mature because the field is plowed up as a homesite for human beings. Or unseasonable frost may kill many insects on a low patch of ground. For some unforeseen reason a bird's territory may prove not to be adequate. And all the surrounding country is held by other members of one's own species—what then does a bird do for food?

He trespasses, and usually the owners of the land where he doesn't belong are lenient. As the season progresses, there is a good deal of this crossing of fence lines. Sometimes the theft of the food is not discovered, for the intruding bird always goes onto a neighbor's property inconspicuously. He stays under the bushes, moves quietly, and of course does not chirp or sing. Even if he is found there, the owner may sing to tell him that he had better go home but will seldom attack and may not

even try to bluff the intruder into retreating. Earlier, at the time the nesting activities were just getting under way, the trespasser would have been chased out indignantly. Occasionally, not often, such disputes result in fatalities. But if slaughter is rare among birds, many species are among the world's best bluffers. Who has not seen the head feathers rise, the body level down, and the open beak make a jab? A threatening bird can look as formidable as a tiny dragon.

Sometimes a whole flock of birds holds and defends a certain area, and this area may be further divided among the individual birds. In flocks of seabirds that nest on shore, the single territory may be only so large that one individual, sitting on eggs, cannot peck the next neighbor; but that square yard of space, or less, is known unerringly to its owner and to the other birds, who respect it. Of the birds that migrate, many scatter when they

reach their southern wintering grounds, fitting themselves in among the local bird population. Since the migrants are mostly different species, they are not treated belligerently. Nevertheless, a few of the species which nest and defend territories in the Northern Hemisphere also claim homesites in their vacationing winter quarters and drive out their fellow travelers.

Occasionally mated female birds help to defend the homesite, but usually they leave that responsibility to the males. Unmated female birds seldom establish territories. Some, not all, unmated males announce boundary lines around plots which they claim as exclusively theirs. Actually, if there were more suitable spaces, many more birds might form family relationships. There have been estimates that in some bird populations as many as 40 per cent are not mated. Their single status is not due in all cases to lack of facilities. Among birds—and mammals

too—there are individuals that simply appear to have no wish to mate. When tested they have proved to be physically sound, with a normal hormonal balance. The reasons for their reluctance are assumed to be psychological. But many birds seem to remain unmated because they fail in the competition for a share of the naturally limited space. This limitation is considered desirable, for the food supply probably would not support a larger number of bird families, and the territorial system is therefore a check on a population explosion of birds.

_____ **Sally Carrighar**

At courtship time, male birds may become feisty. Sage grouse cocks (left) puff out their feathers and spread their tails to lure females and threaten other males. Fights (left, bottom) occasionally erupt. A belligerent Canada gander (above) chases an interloper who trespasses on his territory and attempts to woo his mate.

Matchmaking Among the Birds

There is something about the matchmaking of birds that is not easily penetrated. The jealousies and rivalries of the males and of the females are easily understood,—but those sudden rushes of several males, some of them already mated, after one female, with squeals and screams and great clatter of wings,—what does it mean?

In the latter half of April, we pass through what I call the "robin racket,"—trains of three or four birds rushing pell-mell over the lawn and fetching up in a tree or bush, or occasionally upon the ground, all piping and screaming at the top of their voices. The nucleus of the train is female. One cannot see that the males in pursuit of her are rivals; it seems rather as if they had united to hustle her out of the place. But somehow the matches are no doubt made and sealed during these mad rushes.

Earlier in the season the pretty sparring of the males is the chief feature. You may see two robins apparently taking a walk or a run together over the sward or along the road; only first one bird runs, and then the other. They keep a few feet apart, stand very erect, and the course of each describes the segment of an arc about the other, thus:— 〰〰〰〰. Then, in a twinkling, one makes a spring and they are beak to beak, and claw to claw, as they rise up a few feet into the air. But usually no blow is delivered; not a feather is ruffled; each, I suppose, finds the guard of the other perfect. Then they settle down upon the ground again, and go through with the same running challenge as before.

The bluebird wins his mate by the ardor of his attentions and by finding a house ready built which cannot be surpassed. The male bluebird is usually here several days before the female, and he sounds forth his note as loudly and eloquently as he can till she appears. On her appearance he flies at once to the box or tree cavity upon which he has had his eye, and, as he looks into it, calls and warbles in his most persuasive tones. The contrast in the manners of the two birds is as striking as the contrast in their colors. The male is brilliant and ardent; the female is dim and retiring, not to say indifferent. She may take a hasty peep into the hole in the box or tree and then fly away, uttering a lonesome, homesick note. Only by wooing of many days is she to be fully won.

The matchmaking of the flickers, which often comes under my observation, is in marked contrast to that of the robins and the bluebirds. The male or two males will alight on a limb in front of the female, and go through with a series of bowings and scrapings that are truly comical. He spreads his tail, he puffs out his breast, he

Frigate birds (below) add color to courtship when the male puffs out his bright red throat sac. After staking out nesting sites, the males display their colors to attract females flying overhead. Even after pairing, the male continues his inflated vigil for hours at a time, guarding his mate and the nest until the pair's single egg is laid.

Back braced against his tail, a ruffed grouse (right) fans the air to sound the hollow drumming that attracts his mate. Observers once thought grouse struck their sides or even flapped against a log to create this wooing call. We now know that just the way the wings cup the air produces their curious "bup . . . bup . . up.rrrrr."

Bold gestures and bright displays distinguish different forms of courtship ritual. Among gannets (opposite, assuming a courtship stance), both males and females actively join in the ritual, pursuing each other. Among turkeys, strutting and displaying are reserved for the colorful tom (below, with hen). By season's end, the gannets are nesting in

pairs, but the successful tom has amassed a harem of hens. Color differences also help distinguish the sexes, as in the blue-birds (above), whose iridescent male contrasts with the pale blue-gray female. Some males, like the goldfinch (bottom), undergo a partial molt in spring, casting off winter drabness to reveal a bright courtship plumage.

throws back his head, and then bends his body to the right and to the left, uttering all the while a curious musical hiccough. The female confronts him unmoved, but whether her attitude is critical or defensive, I cannot tell. Presently she flies away, followed by her suitor or suitors, and the little comedy is enacted on another tree.

Among our familiar birds the matchmaking of none other is quite so pretty as that of the goldfinch. The goldfinches stay with us in loose flocks and clad in a dull-olive suit throughout the winter. In May the males begin to put on their bright summer plumage. This is the result of a kind of superficial moulting. Their feathers are not shed, but their dusky covering or overalls are cast off. When the process is only partly completed, the bird has a smutty, unpresentable appearance. But we seldom see them at such times. They seem to retire from society. When the change is complete, and the males have got their bright uniforms of yellow and black, the courting begins. All the goldfinches of a neighborhood collect together and hold a sort of musical festival. The males sing, and the females chirp and call. Whether there is actual competition on a trial of musical abilities of the males before the females or not, I do not know. The best of feeling seems to pervade the company; there is no sign of quarreling or fighting; "all goes merry as a marriage bell," and the matches seem actually to be made during these musical picnics.

I have known the goldfinches to keep up this musical and love-making festival through three consecutive days of a cold northeast rainstorm. Bedraggled, but ardent and happy, the birds were not to be dispersed by weather.

Among all the woodpeckers the drum plays an important part in the matchmaking. The male takes up his stand on a dry, resonant limb, or on the ridgeboard of a building, and beats the loudest call he is capable of. The downy woodpecker usually has a particular branch to which he resorts for advertising his matrimonial wants. A high-hole sends forth a rattle that can be heard a long way off. Then he lifts up his head and utters that long April call, *Wick, wick, wick, wick*. Then he drums again. If the female does not find him, it is not because he does not make noise enough.

All the woodpeckers, so far as I have observed, drum up their mates. The drumming of the male ruffed grouse is for the same purpose; the female hears, concludes to take a walk that way, approaches timidly, is seen and admired, and the match is made. That the male accepts the first female that offers herself is probable. Among all the birds the choice, the selection, seems to belong to the female. The males court promiscuously; the females choose discreetly. What determines the choice of the female would be hard to say. Among songbirds, it is probably the best songster, or the one whose voice suits her taste best. Among birds of bright plumage, it is probably the gayest dress; among the drummers, she is doubtless drawn by some quality of the sound. Our ears and eyes are too coarse to note any differences in these things, but doubtless the birds themselves note differences.

— John Burroughs

A Couple of Pebbles... A Ton of Twigs

It's not surprising that bird nests differ dramatically. Birds themselves vary in size, of course, and in habits. Their enemies differ. Depending on location, available nesting material may change, and so does the climate. Eggs, too, vary in size, in shape and in the number to a clutch. All of these factors have ordained the evolution of a wide variety of nests. Of these, some are spectacular architectural marvels and more than a few are downright exotic.

The matter of size is a good example of this diversity. A hummingbird nest, neatly made of plant down and cobwebs, weighs only a fraction of an ounce. By contrast, an eagle nest, or aerie, may weigh over a ton and be 20 feet tall and 10 feet across.

The largest and most bizarre nest of all is constructed right on the ground by the Australasian megapodes, or mound builders. What they build, really, is a giant incubator. Using their beaks and feet, the 20-inch-long birds scrape dirt and decaying vegetation together into a mound. In dense jungle, where there is little sunlight, the mound may be 35 feet in diameter and 15 feet high. Tunnels up to three feet long are excavated into the mounds and in them the eggs are deposited. Each day, the male comes to the mound and tests the temperature inside with his beak. If it is too cool, he rips the mound apart and adds more decaying vegetable matter. If the temperature is too high, he increases the percentage of sand. Either way, he may move more than a ton of earth.

To most people, "nest" means the familiar cup shape made by passerine, or perching birds. Yet even among these species, some nests hardly fit the conventional mold. The ovenbird is a case in point. A terrestrial warbler from North America, it uses vegetable debris to build a dome-shaped nest on the ground that looks like an old outdoor oven.

In contrast to the ovenbird, the California condor builds practically no nest at all. High in a cave or on a ledge in the mountains of southern California, the condor scrapes a few pebbles or other debris together, on which it lays a single egg every other year.

Far from sunny California, the Adelie penguin does much the same thing. In its antarctic world, however, the pebbles take on a new meaning: the male uses a pebble (probably stolen from another bird's nest) to entice a female into becoming his mate.

Many birds are hole nesters and some must find suitable excavations that have been created by other forces, or other birds. Most of the parrots fit into this category. Unfortunately, the wholesale pet trade hires natives to look for trees with holes in them and chop them down so that the nestlings can be stolen. Every year, the number of places where parrots can nest is being reduced and for some species the danger point has already been reached.

Unique in their own way, swifts use their saliva as basic building material. The nests are usually half-cups in shape and are glued to cave walls, inside hollow trees, chim-

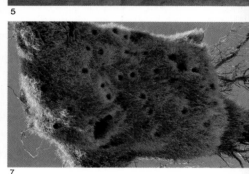

neys, or other surfaces. The African palm swift sticks its nest to the underside of palm leaves; so strong is its saliva-glue that nests almost never fall. The saliva-nest builders produce the only commercially important nest in the world. Those built by cave swiftlets of the genus *Collocalia* form the basis of bird's nest soup, the edible "caviar" of the East.

The dirtiest nest in the world is said to belong to the hoopoe of Eurasia, Africa and Madagascar. Hoopoes are hole-nesters and they will settle for any cavity that they can line with sticks or leaves. While many birds tidy up their nests, hoopoes don't take the trouble. The excretions, and the oils discharged by the female and her chicks when they are alarmed, create a messy nest equaled by few other birds.

The hornbills, found in old-world tropical and subtropical forests, are also odd in their nesting habits. The females wall themselves into a hole in a tree or rocky area and remain there until their chicks are ready to brave the outside world. The males occasionally help the females cement themselves in for what may be more than 100 days of imprisonment. During her incarceration, he brings food, pushing it into a small hole left in the "wall." The female keeps her nest from becoming impossibly foul by high-pressure defecation through a slit left for this purpose.

As their name implies, the old-world weavers fabricate elaborate nests. The weavers reach an acme in the social weaver of southwest Africa. A large tree is chosen and the birds cooperate in the construction of a massive straw roof. Individual nest chambers are then built on the underside of the platform.

The new-world orioles and their relatives weave baggy nests that hang like pendants and may be several feet long. Since these birds, too, are colonial, a single tree may become heavily laden with their nests.

Burrowing owls often take over burrows abandoned by other animals in flat, semi-arid country. Stories about this creature living in the same burrow with rattlesnakes are exaggerated. They only use a burrow if no snakes are in residence.

Some birds do, however, share nests on occasion. In Newcastle, Pennsylvania, for example, a robin and a mourning dove not only incubated their eggs in the same nest for one year, but when the eggs hatched the two birds actually took turns feeding the four chicks.

Although nesting habits have been refined over thousands of years, many birds are remarkably adaptable to the eccentricities of modern living. The prize for adaptability may well go to a pair of rough-winged swallows that nested between the decks of a Tennessee River steamboat. The boat churned back and forth across the river from Guntersville to Hobbs Island. Every day the swallows accompanied the boat on its 24-mile journey in order to feed their young.

Roger Caras

Growing Wings

At hatching, altricial young are scarlet, naked, blind, half-formed distortions of a bird. The body is covered with loose wrinkled skin out of which may arise puffs of grayish down on the back, shoulders, and head. The bird consists of a prominent rear end, a swollen stomach, awkward and feeble legs, fragile wings, and a round soft head. This sleeping life will spend its first ten days in the nest being nursed by its parents. The word altricial derives from the Latin *altrix* meaning nurse.

At hatching, precocial young are covered with buff or gray down, their snappy black eyes are wide open, and they are able to move under their mother in cold weather and into the shade of grasses when the sun is too hot. By the end of the day they follow their guide from the nest. These birds are precocious charmers at hatching. The name precocial comes from the Latin *coquere*, to ripen, and *prae*, before.

Altricial birds hatch in twelve days as half-formed birds who further their development in the nest. Precocial birds hatch after a month as completely formed chicks.

Hatching is an orderly process. When the hatchling first wakes up, it thrusts its bill through the inner membrane to the air sac and begins to breathe. A day later it commences to break out of its prison.

On the tip of the upper bill is a hard white spot called the egg tooth which falls off a few days after hatching. Using its neck muscles the chick rubs the egg tooth against one area of the shell until it weakens and the shell cracks in a star shape. The egg is then pipped. The hatchling rolls a bit to one side and repeats the process, making up to six cracks on the largest circumference. Each crack demands three or four hours of work.

While the parents watch, the bird silently carries on the rest of his battle. Pushing hard with the amazingly strong muscles of his little body, the bird separates the two halves of his shell, so that the wide shallow end rests on his head and neck like a cap and the deeper end encases the rest of his body. Then a few moments of rest when one can see how neatly the shell comes apart.

Three or four minutes later the thrusts are renewed and the bird comes loose from the shell. He rests quietly and unmoving on his side, still two-thirds covered. The next few labors free his legs and his armlike wings. The climax comes with the final thrust when he kicks himself free of the bottom. After another rest he twists his body and flails his limbs until he rolls free of the top as well. Then he curls up as if still in the shell—his bill, wings, and toes all bunched together—and rests on his side.

The shell, containing the hatchling's first white excrement, is carried far from the nest by the parents.

—— **Sarita Van Vleck**

Altricial nestlings, like the naked, one-fifth-ounce wood thrush above and the baby field sparrows at right, are so help- less at birth that they can only raise their heads, open their beaks, and call weakly for food. The eyes of some altricial birds open in 3 days, others take up to 14. Most young spend around 13 days in the nest, but some stay much longer —royal albatross chicks may not leave for 243 days. During their stay in the nest, the babies grow incredibly fast on a largely protein diet. In 3 weeks, a cuckoo gains 50 times its original weight!

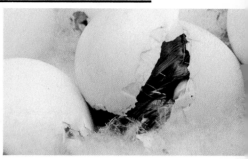

It's "happy landings" when
this wood duck (left) tumbles
out of the egg shell onto the
soft down pulled from its
mother's breast. Note the
pointed egg tooth at the tip of
the bill (left) with which the
hatching infant punctures
chinks in the shell (above, top).
Pushing with its head, neck, and
feet, the bird splits the shell at
the large end and rests before
freeing its feet (middle). Only a
few hours old, these chicks
(bottom) are about to leap
from their nest in a hollow tree
to the ground below and follow
their mother to the water to feed
on marsh plants.

Vanity Has Nothing To Do With Preening

When people "preen," they dress up, primp or generally show off. That's exactly what a bird seems to be doing when it caresses its feathers with its bill. The fact is, however, that the bird is conditioning its feathers as part of the serious business of survival.

Preening is an essential grooming that usually comes after a preliminary dry cleaning or bath. One group of birds that seems to "bathe" and preen at the same time is the heron family. Like other water birds, herons tend to accumulate a coating of slime on their feathers. These birds have three patches of special feathers that break down into a talcumlike powder that is applied to the other feathers by the bill. After the powder absorbs the slime, it is combed out by a specially adapted toe with a comb-like edge.

Preening involves oiling the feathers, as well as cleaning and smoothing them. The oil comes from a special preen gland near the bird's rear. First the creature rubs its bill into the gland, then applies the oil. The oil is a waterproofing compound, and the preen gland is especially well-developed in aquatic birds such as ducks, geese, albatrosses, pelicans, and ospreys.

Like a human with a back itch, a preening bird sometimes needs help getting at those hard-to-reach places around the head. Some species, including pigeons, parakeets and parrots, preen their mates and their young. Some flocking birds, such as penguins, regularly engage in a form of social preening.

Beyond cleaning and conditioning feathers, preening also gets rid of parasites. Some birds just try to scratch them out; others have more ingenious techniques. For example, many birds, including ostriches and a couple of hundred species of perching birds, occasionally resort to a natural pesticide: They sit near an anthill and the ants, sensing an aggressor, crawl aboard and emit formic acid onto the birds' feathers—which drives away mites and other vermin. Other birds pick up ants in their bills and place them where they are most needed, usually the underside of the tips of their primary feathers.

By and large, however, the activity we see and call preening is the end result of a series of events triggered when the bird's body chemistry and nerve endings say it is time to clean and oil those disheveled feathers. Biologically, no bird can afford to let its feathers fall into a state of disrepair, for it needs them for streamlining its angular body and for flight, insulation, skin protection, camouflage and nest building. Yes, it's true: vanity has nothing to do with preening.

— **Bill Vogt**

Feathers, vital for insulation and flight, must be groomed daily to prevent deterioration. Birds like the mallard duck (above) use their bills to coat their feathers with protective oil from a gland near the tail. Some scientists think that a portion of this oil is swallowed during preening, adding vitamin D to the bird's diet. Using its foot, the duck scratches areas that cannot be reached with its bill. Some birds, like the anhinga (opposite), use little oil because their feathers must be water permeable to allow the bird to dive easily for fish. After feeding, anhingas spread their wings to dry and nibble or stroke their feathers to realign the ruffled vanes.

The Wonders of Bird Navigation

As summer approaches, Aristotle wrote, some birds go into hiding, some move from place to place, a few migrate, and others transmute and become different species—the European robin changes into a redstart. For centuries Aristotle's theories were accepted uncritically. Today we know more about birds and migrations and, as our knowledge increases, so does our awe of their seemingly impossible feats.

Despite years of research, we still do not know exactly how birds orient and navigate during their long migrations. However, there are several theories to explain how birds stay on a chosen course, the most common being that birds navigate by the stars and sun. Birds in cages surrounded by mirrors attempt a course based upon where the mirrors indicate the sun is. If they want to fly west, their direction under unobstructed sunlight is westerly, but if the sun is deflected 90° clockwise, west replaces north and they try to head northward. Experiments in planetariums give essentially the same results.

Since the sun and stars shift position season by season, hour by hour, birds must know what time of year and what time of day it is to use them successfully. Even if displaced to an area where the sun takes a totally different path across the sky, some birds seem to know what time it is, where they are and how to get home with uncanny precision.

Some scientists considered the possibility that birds orient themselves using the earth's magnetic field or the Coriolis Effect caused by the earth's rotation. A few believe birds can remember every place they have been and can choose a course based upon this. A larger number, noting that some birds can navigate even on completely overcast days, feel that birds can orient themselves according to the wind's direction. The many avian feats of navigation make the above theories believable. After being released from Boston, Massachusetts, one Manx shearwater journeyed 3,050 miles to its tiny island home off the coast of Wales in 12½ days. Even when removed several thousand miles from their native Midway Island in the center of the Pacific, Laysan albatrosses return home across the featureless ocean.

Some birds travel thousands of miles in their regular migration. The arctic tern travels from one end of the earth to the other. It passes over both the temperate and tropical regions to spend its summers perhaps 300 miles from the North Pole and its winters in Antarctic seas. Of all the land birds the bobolink is the longest-distance migrant, leaving Argentine grasslands for Canadian clover fields on its 7,000-mile migration.

How do migrating birds cover such great distances in such short times? There are several ways: night and even nonstop flight, a faster average air speed during migration, persistence and an ample supply of readily available energy from built-up fat.

Day and night fliers include the golden plover, which makes a 2,400-mile nonstop flight from Nova Scotia to South America in 48 hours. Perhaps one of the most breathtaking feats is that of the tiny ruby-throated hummingbird. After storing an amount of fat equal to almost half their weight they set off from the Texas coast at 50 m.p.h. and cross more than 500 miles of the Gulf of Mexico nonstop.

Birds travel perhaps 10 to 15 m.p.h. faster when migrating than at other times. Although the smaller song birds fly nearly 30 m.p.h. during migration, other birds (including certain ducks, swifts, and plovers) travel at speeds up to 60 m.p.h.

Migrating birds also show a special persistence. If a hawk seizes an individual from a migrating flock, the other birds may not display their usual panic but continue onward.

Nonstop flight, high speed and persistence all require energy and many long-distance migrants build up an ample supply of fat energy before migrating. The New England gunners who slaughtered the now nearly extinct Eskimo curlew gave it the nickname "doughbird" because its tightly stretched breast skin burst when killed birds hit the ground, spattering thick, rich fat.

Migratory birds fly at average altitudes of 4,000 to 6,000 feet. Insect-feeders like swallows and swifts fly below 500 feet where their prey is more plentiful; strong, fast fliers like the shorebirds often travel at high altitudes. Radar readings have shown plovers and sandpipers flying at 20,000 feet. They may be taking advantage of the stable air or prevailing winds.

Migration is the greatest adventure, the hardest trial of a bird's life. Birds cannot predict the storms, squalls, fogs or winds they must encounter. Hundreds of millions may die during migration. But while migration is perilous, its advantages outweigh its disadvantages. It is a key to survival for more than one-third of the world's birds. There is little question that migration is an evolutionary development that has favored the survival of the birds able to meet the demands of an ever changing world.

—Gordon M. Snyder

Canada geese trace a familiar "V" across the sky as they ply a route that can extend from the Gulf of Mexico to Hudson Bay.

Taking a
Closer
Look

The Hunters
of the Moonlight

It was very still in the ricefield. The sawgrass stood stiffly upright, only the flexible tops swaying slightly but giving forth no rustle. Not even an insect hummed and the big bird, standing like a statue near one of the ditch banks, was as motionless as the water at its feet.

The fishing had been very poor that morning. Ardea had spent hours upon the half submerged log near the bank waiting developments. He had the characteristic which marks the true fisherman, unlimited patience, but results were so slow that even this quality was strained. Finally breaking his rigid immobility, he stalked along through the shallows, slipping his feet silently into the water and watching the surface keenly. Even this method proved fruitless and at last he raised his big wings and mounted into the air.

With heavy flappings he alighted at the edge of a misshapen mass of dead sticks up high in a blasted, sun-bleached cypress. Fanning vigorously for a moment, he slowly folded his wings and stared down into the shallow platform which served his family as a home. It was not a handsome home, for it was far from clean and an odor of stale fish clung about it. Neither were its occupants handsome. Half naked, with tufts of feathers sprouting here and there on their skinny bodies, Ardea's youngsters gave little promise of becoming the handsome bird their father was. His arrival, and that of his mate who joined him almost as soon as he alighted, set the little herons into a fever of impatience. Craning necks and bulging eyes, together with half-raised wings, made them seem many more than only four as they clamored for attention. Ardea's mate had evidently been more successful than he, for she stepped into the nest and proceeded to pump the contents of her stomach, a semi-digested mass of fish, into the nearest gaping mouth.

It was not long until the young herons began to show signs of restlessness in their rude home. They had increased astonishingly in size and were awkward and lumbering as they clambered about the branches with the aid of neck and feet. The time had come, however, when they must begin to try their wings. Confidence came quickly once they trusted themselves to the non-supporting element, and they seemed to delight in circling about the nest tree and sailing back and forth to the canals and fishing for themselves. The old herons gradually drifted apart then, and Ardea found much more time available for his own whims and fancies.

This utter freedom of the post-nesting season always returned to him with a pleasing sense of relaxation and relief. It was in this spirit that he journeyed late one afternoon much farther down the tidal river than his usual custom. The sun was sinking as he came to a wide creek which made back through the ricefields to a big swamp, dotted here and there with still lagoons. Ardea wheeled inward from the river and circling one of these quiet expanses in the flooded forest, dropped to the wooded border and stared about him expectantly. It was a beautiful place, the high trees draped with a profusion of gray moss streamers; the still water faithfully reflecting every detail. For some while the old heron stood as motionless as a statue watching the life of the lagoon as it settled for the night.

Coming out of his statuesque pose, he lifted his feet and stalked slowly along the unfamiliar shore, his appetite keen and his eyes busy. Ardea found quickly that he had stumbled upon hunting grounds. His lethal beak darted again and again as he walked, transfixing minnows, frogs and other unwary victims as fast as they appeared. He had been pleasantly engaged for some time when a pale luminance above the trees gave promise of the coming moon, and shortly afterward it climbed above the tree line into a cloudless sky, bathing the lagoon in an elfin, silver light. The old heron ceased his walking as the moonlight grew and stepped upon an ancient log which projected from the trees well out into the still surface. With the coming of the moon, the fishing grew better and better, for even as he stepped upon the log a fish darted out from under it and with a lightning jab of his beak, a slight splash leaped upward as the glittering shape came into the air. Swallowing his catch, Ardea settled on the log, drew his head between his shoulders and lapsed into immobility.

Perhaps it was that little splash, tiny as it was, which attracted the attention of a dweller in the lagoon. Perhaps that dweller had already seen the heron before the latter gained the log, but Ardea did not see those three dark knobs out there on the surface where they were as motionless as could be. Cold, malignant eyes, their vertical pupils blazing with an unwavering intensity, glared upon the feathered fisherman and in their depths was a dull desire, a smouldering flicker of purpose which was unmistakable. The small brain behind those eyes, keen enough when planning attack, demanded action; but for fifteen minutes or more the huge alligator did not move.

Fifty yards separated bird and reptile. Nothing but smooth water lay between them and the old alligator de-

---

Big Cypress Swamp in Florida (left) offers a plentiful food supply and the tall trees common egrets and great blue herons prefer for nesting.

liberated between a direct frontal charge and a cautious circular stalk. Deciding at length upon the latter, those black knobs settled slowly, insensibly beneath the surface. Not a ripple marked their going, not a swirl told where that armored tail had swung the saurian about and headed it toward the trees at a point some distance beyond the unsuspecting heron. Everything was quiet and Ardea still watched the water at his feet.

Under the still radiance of the moon the stalk that followed had something of the uncanny in it. Foot by foot that awful head with the green eyes came nearer. The long ridged tail moved with the complete silence of a shadow, not a ripple stirred the water. Once or twice during that inexorable advance, Ardea plunged his beak downward and each time a tiny splash leaped up and a fish was caught. He began to feel comfortably drowsy and satisfied; one more fish and he would be content to find his roost and sleep until the dawn streaked the Low Country sky. And all the while, slowly, steadily, the long black shape of the alligator neared the log.

Twenty yards from it, the monster came upon another log lying just under the surface. It stopped, the water was too shallow to permit climbing over without some sound; the hunter was still too far for a rush. With infinite stealth and consummate skill, the huge shape backed slightly, circled the obstruction and came at last to the shoreward end of Ardea's stand. Sinking down, it lay for a moment, only the higher ridges of the plated back protruding from the water. Then it seemed to tense suddenly, the loosely swinging tail became rigid and quivered with suppressed energy. Slowly that mighty head came up, huge jaws dropped slightly open showing an array of yellow tusks gleaming against a livid throat. The moonbeams, glancing from the wetly glistening plates of hide, seemed to double the already enormous reptile in size. It appeared gigantic, uncouth, a grisly relic of an age long forgotten. Then it leaped forward.

Totally unaware of the impending doom, Ardea had just speared a frog which swam by the log and had raised his head high and stared out over the lagoon. What fancy sometimes stirs the brain of the wild creatures at crucial moments none can say. Perhaps they come at times of greatest stress, though the import of them may seem nothing more than a sudden impulse. Certain it was that Ardea had no idea of the monster which was stealing upon him from the rear. Perhaps a vision of the old nest tree with his favorite perch flashed across his brain and impelled an answer. Perhaps some shady corner of the ricefield rushed all unheralded to him. All of it, whatever the impression or impulse, lasted but a second. No sooner had he swallowed the frog than, unhurriedly but strongly, Ardea raised his wings and mounted upward just at the identical instant that the alligator charged.

The heavy swishing of his wings filled the air about the heron; and with never a backward glance as he cleared the line of trees in the full brilliance of the moon, the wide-winged Ardea disappeared beyond the cypresses, a blackly moving silhouette against the luminous sky.

Alexander Sprunt, Jr.

A great blue heron moves stealthily through the water but acts with lightning speed when it sees the glint of a fish. Clamping its prey in its beak (below), the heron stretches out its neck and swallows the fish headfirst. Takeoff is awkward for the great blue, but on long flights (far left) it settles into a graceful rhythm with deep wing-beats. Newly hatched herons are fed soft, regurgitated food that is passed from the parent's bill into that of the fledgling (left). Later, whole, fresh fish are left in the nest for the young to eat. Herons nest in crowded colonies, and a single tree may hold many large, untidy, platform-like nests built of sticks and twigs.

Protecting the Nest

A few miles from San Diego, California, there is a ravine known as Tecolote Canyon. The name means "owl," probably handed down from the days of the early Spanish settlers. It was beautiful, for the sides of the canyon were spotted with scrub oak and at the bottom a small stream occasionally broke to the surface and watered a meandering line of sycamores. The owls lived in an abandoned Cooper's Hawk nest, about twenty-five feet from the ground.

The first time I climbed the scrub oak I almost reached the edge of the nest before there was any sign of life. Then from within came a low moan that rapidly intensified into a caterwauling remindful of the battle of angry cats. If I held my position the hideous noise would subside, but at my slightest movement it was instantly repeated.

Finally the face of a Long-eared Owl peered stealth-ily over the edge of the nest. Her pupils, contracted by the light to shoe-button size, stared into mine, which were possibly larger than normal, for I was only a foot away. After minutes of this eye-to-eye showdown I commenced to change position and climb higher. This rewarded me with one of the most beautiful sights I have ever seen in the wild. The female noiselessly extended her wings, raised the feathers to a vertical position and posed as a half circle of mottled mahogany. Although she probably weighed in the neighborhood of a pound, certainly not more, she stood her ground within arm's reach of me, bluffing with every ounce of her small being by assuming a position and size that I admit was terrifying.

On my next visit the owls tried a different technique in their repertoire of many ruses. This time they became secretive and endeavored to blend into the background. One on a broken bough about forty feet from the nest unobtrusively watched my movements through eyelids closed to mere slits. Every feather was clamped to the body, which was held rigidly upright, giving the bird a stick-like appearance. While she watched, two-by-fours, plywood panels, and a seat were lifted to an adjoining branch without a movement from this living statue.

Dusk brought another ruse, the highlight of the show. Now the actors seemed willing to try anything once as I put the finishing touches on the blind that was to hide me for many nights. First an anguished squeaking, like that of a small mammal in distress, drew my attention to a commotion in the grass. As I descended the tree and hurried to investigate, one of the owls flew up in the air only to alight again fifty feet farther on where another battle with an imaginary adversary was staged for my benefit. On and on the bird led me, and if owls have egos, hers was no doubt inflated as I followed willingly.

It was almost dark when I returned to the nest, but the persistent owls were far from through. Lying on one side, an owl would push itself along the ground with a wing alternately flapping and dragging. It was the most brazen fraud I have ever witnessed, even better than that of the Killdeer—the supposed master of the feigned injury.

When I finally broke away to climb to the blind both owls became antagonistic. Every upward step invited dives, and the hurtling bodies of the birds missed me by mere inches. The tops of the scrub oaks formed an almost unbroken blanket of branches, twigs, and leaves, but the agile owls would dive through this maze at a breakneck speed. The attacks of this night were purely a war of nerves, as evidenced by snapping beaks and low moans; but later in the study their dives out of nowhere were miraculously silent and really carried authority. After my head had been gashed a few times by raking talons, I came to the conclusion that safety was better than valor and thereafter I walked to and from the nest with a leafy branch held above me.

Lewis Wayne Walker

Wide-eyed and menacing, a long-eared owl (opposite) strikes threatening postures to intimidate intruders. Changing its normal stance (top left), the owl enhances its size by spreading its wings and tail feathers (left) before launching itself for a savage attack (top right).

Baker's Blue-Jay Yarn

Animals talk to each other, of course. There can be no question about that; but I suppose there are very few people who can understand them. I never knew but one man who could. I knew he could, however, because he told me so himself. He was a middle-aged, simple-hearted miner, who had lived in a lonely corner of California, among the woods and mountains, a good many years, and had studied the ways of his only neighbors, the beasts and birds, until he could accurately translate any remark which they made. This was Jim Baker. According to Jim Baker, some animals have only a limited education and use very simple words, and scarcely ever a comparison or a flowery figure; whereas, certain other animals have a large vocabulary, a fine command of language and a ready and fluent delivery; consequently these latter talk a great deal; they like it. Baker said that, after long and careful observation, he had come to the conclusion that the blue-jays were the best talkers he had found among the birds and beasts. Said he:

"There's more *to* a blue-jay than any other creature. He has got more moods and more different kinds of feelings than other creatures; and, mind you, whatever a blue-jay feels, he can put into language. And no mere commonplace language, either, but rattling, out-and-out book-talk—and bristling with metaphor, too—just bristling! And as for command of language—why, *you* never see a blue-jay get stuck for a word. No man ever did. They just boil out of him! And another thing: I've noticed a good deal, and there's no bird, or cow, or anything that uses as good grammar as a blue-jay. You may say a cat uses good grammar. Well, a cat does—but you let a cat get excited, once; you let a cat get to pulling fur with another cat on a shed, nights, and you'll hear grammar that will give you the lockjaw. Ignorant people think it's the *noise* which fighting cats make that is so aggravating, but it ain't so; it's the sickening grammar they use. Now I've never heard a jay use bad grammar but very seldom; and when they do, they are as ashamed as a human; they shut right down and leave.

"You may call a jay a bird. Well, so he is, in a measure—because he's got feathers on him, and don't belong to no church, perhaps, but otherwise he is just as much a human as you be. And I'll tell you for why. A jay's gifts, and instincts, and feelings, and interests cover the whole ground. A jay hasn't got any more principle than a Congressman. A jay will lie, a jay will steal, a jay will deceive, a jay will betray; and, four times out of five, a jay will go back on his solemnest promise. Now, on top of all this, there's another thing: a jay can out-swear any gentleman in the mines. You think a cat can swear. Well, a cat can; but you give a blue-jay a subject that calls for his reserve powers, and where is your cat? Don't talk to *me*—I know too much about this thing. And there's yet another thing: in the one little particular of scolding—just good, clean, out-and-out scolding—a blue-jay can lay over anything, human or divine. Yes, sir, a jay is everything that a man is. A jay can cry, a jay can laugh, a jay can feel shame, a jay can reason and plan and discuss, a jay likes gossip and scandal, a jay has got a sense of humor, a jay knows when he is an ass just as well as you do—maybe better. If a jay ain't human, he better take in his sign, that's all. Now I am going to tell you a perfectly true fact about some blue-jays.

"When I first begun to understand jay language correctly, there was a little incident happened here. Seven years ago, the last man in this region but me moved away. There stands his house—been empty ever since; a log house, with a plank roof—just one big room, and no more; no ceiling—nothing between the rafters and the floor. Well, one Sunday morning I was sitting out here in front of my cabin with my cat, taking the sun, and looking at the blue hills, when a blue-jay lit on that house, with an acorn in his mouth, and says, 'Hello, I reckon I've struck something.' When he spoke the acorn fell out of his mouth and rolled down the roof, of course, but he didn't care; his mind was all on the thing he had struck. It was a knot-hole in the roof. He cocked his head to one side, shut one eye and put the other to the hole, like a 'possum looking down a jug; then he glanced up with his bright eyes, gave a wink or two with his wings—which signifies gratification, you understand—and says, 'It looks like a hole, it's located like a hole—blamed if I don't believe it *is* a hole!'

"Then he cocked his head down and took another look; he glances up perfectly joyful this time; winks his wings and his tail both, and says, 'Oh, no, this ain't no fat thing, I reckon! If I ain't in luck—why, it's a perfectly elegant hole!' So he flew down and got that acorn, and fetched it up and dropped it in, and was just tilting his head back with the heavenliest smile on his face, when all of a sudden he was paralyzed into a listening attitude, and that smile faded gradually out of his countenance like breath off'n a razor, and the queerest look of surprise took its place. Then he says, 'Why, I didn't hear it fall!' He cocked his eye at the hole again and took a long look; raised up and shook his head; stepped around to the other side of the hole, and took another look

Twain's blue-jay story adds credence to the old adage that truth is stranger than fiction. Jim Baker's blue-jay spent only one day dropping acorns through a knothole into a deserted cabin, but real birds—woodpeckers— have been observed doing exactly that for months, until a more compelling urge finally overcame their hoarding instinct.

from that side; shook his head again. He studied a while, then he just went into the *details*—walked round and round the hole, and spied into it from every point of the compass. No use. Now he took a thinking attitude on the comb of the roof, and scratched the back of his head with his right foot a minute, and finally says, 'Well, it's too many for *me*, that's certain; must be a mighty long hole; however, I ain't got no time to fool around here; I got to 'tend to business; I reckon it's all right— chance it, anyway!'

"So he flew off and fetched another acorn and dropped it in, and tried to flirt his eye to the hole quick enough to see what become of it, but he was too late. He held his eye there as much as a minute; then he raised up and sighed, and says, 'Confound it, I don't seem to understand this thing, no way; however, I'll tackle her again.' He fetched another acorn, and done his level best to see what become of it, but he couldn't. Then he begun to get mad. He held in for a spell, walking up and down the comb of the roof, and shaking his head and muttering to himself; but his feelings got the upper hand of him presently, and he broke loose and cussed himself black in the face. I never see a bird take on so about a little thing. When he got through, he walks to the hole and looks in again for half a minute; then he says, 'Well, you're a long hole, and a deep hole, and a mighty singular hole altogether—but I've started to fill you, and I'm d-d if I *don't* fill you, if it takes a hundred years!'

And with that, away he went. You never see a bird work so since you was born . . . the way he hove acorns into that hole for about two hours and a half was one of the most exciting and astonishing spectacles I ever struck. He never stopped to take a look any more —he just hove 'em in, and went for more. Well, at last he could hardly flop his wings, he was so tuckered out. He comes a-dropping down, once more, sweating like an ice-pitcher, drops his acorn in and says, '*Now* I guess I've got the bulge on you by this time!' So he bent down for a look. If you'll believe me, when his head come up again he was just pale with rage. He says, 'I've shoveled acorns enough in there to keep the family thirty years, and if I can see a sign of one of 'em, I wish I may land in a museum with a belly full of sawdust in two minutes!'

"He just had strength enough to crawl up on to the comb and lean his back agin the chimbly, and then he collected his impressions and begun to free his mind. I see in a second that what I had mistook for profanity in the mines was only just the rudiments, as you may say.

"Another jay was going by, and heard him doing his devotions, and stops to inquire what was up. The sufferer told him the whole circumstance, and says, 'Now, yonder's the hole, and if you don't believe me, go and look for yourself.' So this fellow went and looked, and comes back and says, 'How many did you say you put in there?' 'Not any less than two tons,' says the sufferer. The other jay went and looked again. He couldn't seem to make it out, so he raised a yell, and three more jays come. They all examined the hole, they all made the sufferer tell it over again, then they all discussed it, and got as many leather-headed opinions about it as an average crowd of humans could have done.

"They called in more jays; then more and more, till pretty soon this whole region 'peared to have a blue flush about it. There must have been five thousand of them; and such another jawing and disputing and ripping and cussing, you never heard. Every jay in the whole lot put his eye to the hole, and delivered a more chuckle-headed opinion about the mystery than the jay that went there before him. They examined the house all over too. The door was standing half-open, and at last one old jay happened to go and light on it and look in. Of course, that knocked the mystery galley-west in a second. There lay the acorns, scattered all over the floor. He flopped his wings and raised a whoop. 'Come here!' he says, 'Come here, everybody; hang'd if this fool hasn't been trying to fill up a house with acorns!' They all came a-swooping down like a blue cloud, and as each fellow lit on the door and took a glance, the whole absurdity of the contract that that first jay had tackled hit home, and he fell over backward with laughter, and the next jay took his place and done the same.

"Well, sir, they roosted around here on the housetop and the trees for an hour, and guffawed over that thing like human beings. It ain't no use to tell me a blue-jay hasn't got a sense of humor, because I know better. And memory, too. They brought jays here from all over the United States to look down that hole, every summer for three years. Other birds, too. And they could all see the point, except an owl that come from Nova Scotia to visit the Yo Semite, and he took this thing in on his way back. He said he couldn't see anything funny in it. But then, he was a good deal disappointed about Yo Semite, too."

Mark Twain

Nature's Little Dynamos

BLUE-THROATED HUMMINGBIRD

LONG-TAILED SYLPH HUMMINGBIRD

Hummingbirds feeding on the wing hang nearly motionless as they lap up nectar through probing bills. This helicopter-like hovering is made possible by the structure and motion of their tiny wings. The flat, rigid wings move only at the shoulder, enabling the birds to twist and turn them back and forth freely in almost any direction.

CALLIOPE HUMMINGBIRD

Perhaps the most extraordinary thing about the hummingbird is its power plant. Hummingbirds have the highest energy output per unit of weight of any living warm-blooded animal. In discussing their extraordinary activity, figures are fairly meaningless unless they can be related to something we all recognize. For that reason I will use humans as a standard of reference — not a valid scientific comparison, perhaps, but one which will be understandable.

A hummingbird while hovering has an energy output per unit weight about ten times that of a man running nine miles an hour. This is pretty close to the highest possible output of human energy and a pace that can be maintained no longer than half an hour. A hummingbird can fly for much longer periods. A man doing the same work per unit weight would be expending 40 horsepower!

A man's actual daily energy output is about 3,500 calories. The daily output of a hummingbird leading its ordinary life — eating, flying, perching, sleeping — if calculated for a 170-pound man is equivalent to about 155,000 calories.

If we convert these figures to food intake the results are astonishing. A normal man will consume two to two and a half pounds of food per day. If his energy output were that of a hummingbird, he would have to consume during the day 285 pounds of hamburger, or 370 pounds of boiled potatoes, or 130 pounds of bread!

Actually hummingbirds use sugar as their principal food and sugar has a much higher energy content than any of the items listed here for the human larder. Even so the average hummingbird consumes half its weight of sugar daily, an extraordinary intake.

Hummingbirds must feed abundantly and regularly to keep up their energy supply. If artificial feeders are provided, they come in for their snack once every ten or fifteen minutes. We humans can get along on a charge of fuel three times a day — hummingbirds, relatively speaking, must refuel almost continuously.

After all this, it might well be asked what they do at night. Here Nature, with her customary ingenuity, has found an unusually elegant solution. She has given the birds the ability to pass into a state of suspended animation, during which the body temperature drops and the energy output sinks to a very low figure. In this state the birds can be handled without their taking the slightest notice. The factors inducing them to enter this torpid condition are not yet completely understood. Confusingly, it is not a nightly occurrence, nor is it necessarily associated with low temperatures.

My own view is that passage into torpor is in some way connected with the energy reserves of the bird at nightfall. If, for example, the bird has fed well during the day and its energy reserves are high, it will sleep normally. If, however, food is scarce and our bird goes to its slumber without sufficient nourishment, it will stretch out its available energy reserves by becoming torpid. Arousal from the torpid state is extremely rapid and almost before you know it the birds are wide awake and eager for their morning meal.

— **Crawford H. Greenewalt**

One Day at Teton Marsh

This was the Osprey's first autumn. He may have had no sure sense, yet, of the change he must make with the season's changing. On this day in September, however, the sky above Jackson Hole no longer seemed large enough for him. At least it was no longer large enough to share.

Head lowered between his shoulders, the Osprey watched another hawk, a harrier, hunting over the marsh below. Many times that harrier had invaded his tree to challenge him, but the Osprey's parents always had been there to drive him out. For a week they had been gone. Sometime the young fish hawk must humble the harrier —on this day! Now, while the other one hovered over the Varying Hare.

Crying out his intention, the Osprey swung from his bough. The harrier looped up, gained the higher level, spread his talons, and plunged for the Osprey's back. The Osprey shot from under him, wheeled, and spiraled over the harrier. The harrier gave himself to an eddy of wind, rose with it, turned to face the oncoming Osprey, drained the last lift from the gust, and passed on the upper side. As the two met, he raked a claw through the Osprey's wing. The Osprey banked to drive back at him, but the harrier broke from the fight at his instant of victory. He sank away, and the Osprey returned to his tree.

The sheer-sided basin was a valley to please an osprey, for all these hawks are attracted by heights; everywhere they build their nests on the tallest trees or near enough so they can perch on them. Below they must have the shine of water, shot with the glint of fish. The Osprey had found that, too. His nest was out on the valley floor, and water was all around it. A crease down the plain, choked with trees, led the Snake River past. And flowing in from the Grand Teton came Cottonwood Creek. In the angle between the creek and the river, the beavers had formed the marsh.

But now the marsh looked strange. As the beaver dam had washed away, the water had drained from the side channels, which now were muddy troughs with banks of exposed, white, matted roots. Water still lay in the lower end, but its level had dropped so that the door of the beaver house was revealed.

He hovered above the beaver house, peering into the sticks at its base, home of the large Trout, as he knew. A scream—the harrier's—struck from his left. The Osprey sheered toward his attacker. The two would have met over the shore of the pond, but the Osprey went into a dive. For up from the brush, with an airy deadliness, swung another hawk, the young harrier's mother.

Checking his plunge, the Osprey skimmed under them. They turned in a down-curve so steep they were flung half-over, and straightened, and pressed ahead. The Osprey led into the cottonwoods separating the pond from the plain. He tried to lose them by weaving among the boughs. But the harriers, pursuers of dodging prey, seemed to foresee his moves. Their screams were upon him. They were short-cutting now. He could escape only in a long level flight. He swung away up the river. The harriers knew as quickly when they had lost. Behind the Osprey their cries grew faint; then ceased. The Osprey turned down again and stopped on the island across from the marsh.

Something white dropped on the branch beside him. At once his head was erect, and he discovered that many of the white flakes were falling. They tumbled and swirled, a cloud in fragments, a cloud of vagrant, disordered white scraps. Between them the air looked gray. Soon the mountains had vanished behind a nearer wall. The plain was becoming white, seen through a web of white boughs. On the opposite bank of the river he could see the marsh willows, now misty gold sprays.

Late in the day hunger drove him out of the island tree into the snow. He stayed low enough to keep his landmarks in sight, and flew toward the pond. But there no

The Snake River winds through Grand Teton National Park, home of the osprey (above) swooping down to pluck fish from the chilled rapids.

longer was much pond. A muddy hollow had a rivulet draining the center.

He searched in the rivulet for fish. None was in it. The Osprey flew from end to end of the desolate new swale, turned then abruptly toward the river.

He never had caught a fish in the river. He had seen his parents do it, but even they had preferred to take their food from the pond. Knowledge inherited by his nerves sent him to the center of the current, where he discovered a whitefish.

Keeping the fish in sight, the hawk spiraled upward. To drive himself deep enough into the water, he must begin his plunge at least from treetop level. But when he reached that height, he could not see the fish. Everything below him was blurred by the snow. A prolonged snowfall would make his kind of hunting impossible.

Through the rest of the afternoon he perched on the island. The cloud of snowflakes thinned; then, with nothing to make its end noticeable, was gone. A gray density still hung overhead, but high in the west it dissolved suddenly, and the Teton peaks appeared.

The Osprey would try again to catch a fish in the river. He flew upstream and back, frequently dipping for a closer view. The flow was so rapid that he scarcely could steady his gaze upon it. Nothing retarded this river; nothing broke it into foam. The movement had a look of swift brutal force, a capturing pull.

But soon the Osprey found a Trout. This one was poised at the edge of the current, where the flow passed the quiet water enclosed by a curve in the bank. The Osprey beat his way higher, took his position above the Trout. Then he flung up his wings and made his steep strike. He caught the fish with both claws, sank until he was wholly submerged, and was drawn out into the current. He never before had felt its power. It enclosed him in tumult. But the river was water, like the pond. His wings knew what to do. They swung downward, and the hawk's dive was stopped.

He had not yet broken the surface when the wings, clutching together under him, reached their lowest point. The wings came up and began to beat. But opposed to their lifting was the drag of the river. And the Osprey had caught too large a fish, in his inexperience, adding too much to his weight. The Trout was trying to dive into deeper water. Its thrashing had locked the Osprey's talons into its bones. Again the long wings drew together below the hawk, but he did not rise to the top of the water, not high enough even to snatch a breath.

As he struggled, he was swept toward the mouth of Cottonwood Creek. Just above that point a dead willow, drifting down, had caught on the bank. Half-submerged, it floated there securely. The Osprey struck on the sweeper, was held against it briefly, was pushed out by an eddy, seemed to be swinging away, but was stopped again when the longest branch slid beneath his wing.

Now the clean, brown and white bird was wreckage among the muddy leaves, grass, and twigs snagged by the willow. When one of the current's cradles reached him, the soaked feathers of his head rose above the surface but at once were submerged again. The Trout wrestled in the loose claws. Torn but alive, it worked itself free. The Osprey did not know. As soon as his talons were empty, they folded in, limp. The ripples began to slap one inert foot against the branch.

The harrier discovered the Osprey. Swinging along the bank in his hunting, he glimpsed the white head in the water's sweep. His sharp, high scream was like talons piercing. The cries that followed might have been the attacks of a ravenous beak. That was always the cadence of the harrier's taunts—a shrill threat breaking into impatient gibes. The Osprey had heard it many times.

The closed eyes did not open, and the claws of the Osprey did not twitch. But the wild ones are not deceived about death. The harrier must have sensed that under the numb brain of the fish hawk some valor of flesh was fighting. Though he could not enter the water, the harrier continued to strike his enemy with his voice.

That voice had roused the energy of the young Osprey each time that it stirred his parents to a chase. Twice that very day, the sound had stimulated a surge of strength. The harrier might more nearly have defeated his rival if he had flown away, silent, leaving in the Osprey's ears and the depths of his spirit only the vast indifference of the water's roar.

But he remained, screaming, above the willow sweeper. And then once when the Osprey's claw struck the bough, it took hold. Slowly the feet lifted the great wet bird until he was out of the water and up in the willow's clustered boughs, above the river. He rested there with his wings spread and his feathers fluffed to dry. A weak shake, another more vigorous, rid the feathers of some of the water's weight. Between these attempts the Osprey was quiet, gathering and pointing his energy, a skill practiced many times before dives.

The harrier still tormented him, but not so constantly. That hawk was watching for some careless creature to expose itself on the canals of the marsh. Various animals had prowled there before the snow fell. The harrier, hoping for more of them, was forgetting caution.

The instant came when the Osprey's wings could lift him. He stretched and lowered them several times; then hovered over the willow, not quite secure. He crossed to the island. His next exercise was a flight up its shore.

The harrier was gliding over the river, just lower than the tops of the bank willows. Now he was facing downstream. From the island's northern tip came the Osprey, riding the riverwind, sweeping toward him with motionless wings. When he was near, he cried a warning, and the harrier swerved but not quickly enough. The Osprey dived upon him, and a blow from his claw on the harrier's head sent the harrier reeling over, stunned. He hit the water. Instantly it snared his capsized wings. With no chance to right himself, the harrier was carried down on his back into the tumbling currents where Cottonwood Creek joined the river.

———— Sally Carrighar

This young osprey represents only one of perhaps dozens of generations to emerge from the same treetop nest over a period of up to 40 years.

Listening Point

The canoe was drifting off the islands, and the time had come for the calling, that moment of magic in the north when all is quiet and the water still iridescent with the fading glow of sunset. Even the shores seemed hushed and waiting for that first lone call, and when it came, a single long-drawn mournful note, the quiet was deeper than before.

Above came a swift whisper of wings, and as the loons saw us they called wildly in alarm, increased the speed of their flight, and took their laughing with them into the gathering dusk. Then came the answers we had been waiting for, and the shores echoed and re-echoed until they seemed to throb with the music. This was the symbol of the lake country, the sound that more than any other typifies the waters and forests of the wilderness.

While the northern loon in startling black and white, with its necklace of silver and jet and five-foot spread of wings, is of great interest scientifically, it is the calling that all remember. Whoever has heard it during spring and summer never forgets the wild laughing tremolo of the reverberating choruses.

One such night is burned into my memory. It was moonlight, the ice had just gone out, and the spring migration was in full swing. Loons were calling everywhere, not only on Knife but on adjacent lakes, and the night was full of their music from sunset until dawn. The echoes kept the calling going until it was impossible at times to tell which was real.

The weirdest call of all is the yodel somewhat similar to the break in voice and the clear bugle-like note used when a canoe is approaching a nesting area or when invasion is imminent. It can start all the loons within hearing, and when the yodeling blends with tremolo they are really making music.

The third call is the wail often mistaken for the howl of a wolf, and of much the same quality. It rises and falls in pitch and is used when a mate is calling for relief from its brooding on the nest or when signaling the young. Just that morning we heard it among the islands. We had been watching a pair swim slowly around the little bay where they had nested, with a lone chick riding sedately upon the back of one of them. When they saw us, they gave their warning calls at once, for that lone chick riding so grandly around the bay and no more than a day or two off the nest was too small to fend for itself.

Just after the ice was out we had watched that pair come into the bay, stake out their nesting area, and repel invaders whenever they approached. One day we watched the courtship. They came toward each other

slowly and, as they neared, dipped their bills rapidly in the water and just as rapidly flipped them out again. This was followed by several short swift dives, exaggerated rolling preens and stretchings such as only loons seem able to do. Suddenly they broke away from such intimacy, raced off across the water, striking the surface with powerful wing beats in a long curving path that eventually led back to where they had started. All during this time they indulged in the laughing call. Sometimes in the ecstasy of display they reared high on their tails as they did when their chick was endangered, struck their snowy breasts violently on the water, then raced again around the bay. Only once did we see this, but shortly afterward the mating was over and then we found the nest in a tussock of grass on a little swampy island close to shore and facing the open water. It was placed so they could slip off swiftly and reach the deeps should danger come behind them from the shore. The two olive-brown and somewhat speckled eggs were soon laid in a small shallow depression in the grass that was built up during the days of incubation until it was a concave little mound, each mate doing its share while it sat there, pecking and adding a grass blade at a time from the vegetation within reach.

A couple of weeks later one of the eggs was destroyed by some prowler, possibly a mink, a crow or a muskrat. The remaining egg now took all of the loons' attention, and they guarded it jealously every moment of the day and night. If this had been stolen too, it would have meant a new nest and possibly another hatching.

Scientists say that in half the nests only one hatches out, and that the low rate of survival accounts for the fact that loons are never numerous. If two individuals reproduce themselves after their third year, then things are going well. It is surprising in view of the high mortality rate that populations remain as steady as they do, that, in spite of predation, loons are found on almost every lake in the north.

One afternoon we sat on the point watching a flock of loons playing on the open water. They had been there as a group since midsummer, bachelor loons and pairs that had not nested or had lost their eggs. Now free of responsibilities, these thwarted birds gathered each morning and spent the day together in the open.

A pair flew close to the point and settled in the bay off the beach, and we watched them diving there for min-

In the stillness of dawn, a canoeist on a northern lake (right) is apt to hear only the plaintive call of a loon to its mate.

Because she is awkward and slow-moving on land, a mother loon builds her nest as close to the water as possible (right). If danger threatens her on the shore, she can slide quickly into the lake and escape. Loon chicks can swim at birth but tire easily the first few weeks and often rest by riding on their parents' backs (opposite).

nows, timing them to see how long they could stay submerged. Seldom did one stay under for more than half a minute, but there are records of dives as long as two and three minutes in duration. Some have been recorded even longer than that, but such observers may have failed to see a partial emergence for air. They are wonderful divers and swimmers, can pursue and overtake the swiftest of fish, and it has been said a loon can dive at the flash of a gun and be under water before the bullet strikes.

They can also submerge gradually, can control specific gravity possibly by a compression of feathers and expulsion of air from the lungs until the body is approximately the same weight as the water. All divers have a high tolerance for carbon dioxide, and oxygen needs are met, not from free air in the lungs, but from the oxyhemoglobin and oxymyoglobin stored in the muscles, substances responsible for the dark color of flesh in most waterfowl. This explains the diving, the gradual sinking from sight, and the fact that they have been caught on fishermen's set lines in Lake Superior at depths of two hundred feet.

Once I sat in a canoe at Lower Basswood Falls and watched a loon fishing in the rapids not fifty feet away. Suddenly the bird dove and swam directly under the canoe not two feet below the surface. The wings were held tightly at the sides and the legs the sole means of locomotion. When a young chick is learning to swim beneath the surface it uses both legs and wings, a reversion perhaps to the days of its reptilian ancestors; a habit generally abandoned, however, when it becomes adult.

It was now much too dark to see and we left our loons for the light and warmth of the cabin, but in the morning we watched them again. The pair had stayed close to the bay during the night and now were swimming around in the sunshine, getting ready to join the gathering flock on the open lake. We watched them, the brilliant black-and-white markings on their backs, saw one preen, rolling over on its side exposing the silvery-white breast until it glittered and shone in the morning sun. The other rose to its full height, flapped its wings vigorously, and settled down again. Then both dove with scarcely a ripple to mark their descent and soon were far past the point, heading for the rendezvous.

A pair flew overhead, and we heard plainly the whistle of their wings, watched the slow and powerful beats as they headed across the lake. As they passed the gathering flock they gave the tremolo once and then settled down with the rest. I had hoped they might do what I had seen them do in the past, glide into the waiting group with wings set and held in a motionless V above their backs.

Once I had seen them come in that way on Kekekabic, approaching the lake like seaplanes about to land in a long unbroken glide from the ridge to the water's surface.

But, while they are strong flyers and can swim and dive as few birds can, they are absolutely helpless on land, and only once have I seen one more than twenty feet from water. I was coming across a portage with a canoe on my back, and there, to my amazement, was a loon standing bolt upright in the center of the trail. I was so startled by the apparition in black and white that its scream of alarm almost made me drop the canoe. The bird turned and literally hurled itself toward the shore, half flying, swimming and running on its ridiculously tiny legs. With a wild water-choked yelp it plunged into the shallows and out to diving depth and swiftly disappeared. That explained why nests are always so close to shore. Loons must be able to slide instantly into the water. No creature is clumsier out of its element than this great diver of the north.

The sound of a whippoorwill means an orange moon coming up in the deep south; the warbling of meadowlarks the wide expanses of open prairies with the morning dew still upon them; the liquid notes of a robin before a rain the middle west and east; the screaming of Arctic terns the marshes of the far north. But when I hear the wild rollicking laughter of a loon, no matter where I happen to be, it means only one place in the world to me—the wilderness lake country and Listening Point.

Sigurd F. Olson

The Gloomiest Bird

The creature called the turkey buzzard hovers over the land like a fallen angel. A great carrion bird with a naked, raddled head and plumage like an old shroud, watching for death with his amazing eyes.

Other birds and animals do not fear him, for unlike his raptor cousins he does not bring death; he only attends it. Somewhere along the antediluvian track he specialized, losing his raptorial talons and the killing power of his feet. When the buzzard lost his ability to kill and embraced a post-mortem cuisine, he became the the most despised of birds.

He is certainly the ugliest. Not just homely, but repugnant in an epic, classic way. He's the Ugly Champ of America, hands down. His feathers are a rusty black edged with brown and his only color is in the naked atrocity of a head.

Yet, for all his graveyard look, he is among the most beautiful of birds on the wing. Few other American birds possess such majesty of flight. He leaves all ugliness on the earth below, and after the first wing strokes as he labors heavily away from his carrion—and as he earns enough altitude to find the thermal updrafts and the high, tending winds—he becomes a floating mote of infinite grace.

His broad, gloomy wings may span six feet, but he is not heavy. I once picked up a dead buzzard that had been shot by a hunter. The bird was in good condition and full flesh, but weighed only five pounds. While in flight the primaries of his wing tips are spread like fingers and the head and neck are snugged in close to the body. From a distance he may appear almost headless, and unlike the eagles—with which he is often confused —his tail is never spread in flight.

A turkey buzzard has an air about him, and in my experience he is easily the raunchiest, ripest creature that breathes. Part of this is caused by certain natural oils in his plumage, and part by his feeding and nesting habits. Whatever it is, I only know that a buzzard stinks to high heaven and no one but a case-hardened biologist can stand to investigate him closely.

Some years ago, a friend of mine moved in with a family of buzzards in an Ozark cave to escape a thunderstorm. In short order he became a vulture expert.

When a buzzard is gorged with carrion, he may be too heavy for a quick takeoff in an emergency. So he just salvoes his payload by regurgitating until he's light enough to fly. This nervous response to danger is also a defense, and both young and old buzzards can vomit accurately and forcefully when frightened. That's what

With telescopic vision, a turkey vulture can see its next meal even while soaring a mile above the earth (opposite, middle). In the relentless search for food, a vulture, sitting like a totem atop a saguaro cactus, is soon joined by others (left). At night the gregarious birds often roost together in trees (opposite, bottom).

my friend learned in that Ozark cave, although it was a couple of years before he could bear to speak of it and he never did manage to be objective about the affair.

Repugnant as the vultures seem to us, they are superbly adapted to their way of life. They have some of the most splendid eyes in nature. A vulture can mark a dead rabbit in a field when the bird is nearly out of sight in a blank sky. The great wings are constructed for tireless soaring, and the beak is designed for tearing flesh, with outer nostrils passing entirely through the beak and the inner nostrils opening from within the beak. This prevents clogging of the nostrils by food, and the featherless head is easily kept clean when plunged into the depths of a putrescent carcass.

The vulturine digestive tract must be sheathed with tool steel, for it can withstand powerful toxins that are lethal to most other warm-blooded creatures.

One of the most potent natural poisons known is the metabolic by-product of the bacterium *Clostridium botulinus*. The toxin of one of this bacterium's types is responsible for the sweeping botulism plagues that kill hundreds of thousands of ducks at a whack. The chemicals produced by this tiny germ cause a form of violent food poisoning—a sort of super ptomaine. Yet, the turkey vulture can resist a dose of *botulinus* toxin that will kill 300,000 guinea pigs.

So if it's dead, the turkey vulture can safely eat it. The big birds are a prized sanitation corps down south, for a flock of the birds can reduce a dead cow to shining bones in a few days. A southern farmer seldom needs to bury dead stock, but just drags it to some remote corner of his place and forgets about it. The vultures take over from there.

In old Charleston, buzzards once roamed the streets, cleaning up any refuse that was edible. There, as in most parts of the country, it was not only against the law to kill vultures but also against public opinion. The big birds harm neither domestic stock, wildlife, nor man's interests.

Primitive man still regards the vulture as a messmate, although modern man reviles the bird because of its table manners and diet. This is only one of the affectations we've developed since we've moved out of the woods and uptown, for it hasn't been long since our kinfolks dined with vultures from the same ripening carcasses.

We're older now, and more polished. We know what's good for us and we eat our fresh meat and vegetables. But the buzzard still clings to his foul carrion fare, gives us a sepulchral horselaugh, and lives to a ripe old age!

John Madson

A water ouzel perches on a rock (top) in a rushing mountain stream before diving in (bottom) to look for insect larvae on the stony bottom. Having found a juicy grub, the ouzel flies through a waterfall (middle) to its nest upstream. This sprightly robin-sized bird lives along streams in western mountains from Alaska to Panama.

Bird of Blooming Waters

The waterfalls of the Sierra are frequented by only one bird—the ouzel or water thrush. He is a singularly joyous and lovable little fellow, about the size of a robin, clad in a plain waterproof suit of bluish gray, with a tinge of chocolate on the head and shoulders. In form he is about as smoothly plump and compact as a pebble that has been whirled in a pot-hole, the flowing contour of his body being interrupted only by his strong feet and bill, the crisp wing-tips, and the up-slanted wren-like tail.

Among all the countless waterfalls I have met in the course of ten years' exploration in the Sierra, whether among the icy peaks, or warm foot-hills, or in the profound yosemitic cañons of the middle region, not one was found without its ouzel. No cañon is too cold for this little bird, none too lonely, provided it be rich in falling water. Find a fall, or cascade, or rushing rapid, anywhere upon a clear stream, and there you will surely find its complementary ouzel, flitting about in the spray, diving in foaming eddies, whirling like a leaf among beaten foam-bells; ever vigorous and enthusiastic, yet self-contained, and neither seeking nor shunning your company.

He is the mountain streams' own darling, the hummingbird of blooming waters, loving rocky ripple-slopes and sheets of foam as a bee loves flowers, as a lark loves sunshine and meadows. Among all the mountain birds, none has cheered me so much in my lonely wanderings, —none so unfailingly. For both in winter and summer he sings, sweetly, cheerily, independent alike of sunshine and of love, requiring no other inspiration than the stream on which he dwells. While water sings, so must he, ever attuning his voice in sure accord.

What may be regarded as the separate songs of the ouzel are exceedingly difficult of description, because they are so variable and at the same time so confluent. Though I have been acquainted with my favorite ten years, and during most of this time have heard him sing nearly every day, I still detect notes and strains that seem new to me.

The more striking strains are perfect arabesques of melody, composed of a few full, round, mellow notes, embroidered with delicate trills which fade and melt in long slender cadences. In a general way his music is that of the streams refined and spiritualized. The deep booming notes of the falls are in it, the trills of rapids, the gurgling of margin eddies, the low whispering of level reaches, and the sweet tinkle of drops oozing from the ends of mosses and falling into tranquil pools.

His food, as far as I have noticed, consists of all kinds of water insects, which in summer are chiefly procured along shallow margins. Here he wades about ducking his head under water and deftly turning over pebbles and fallen leaves with his bill, seldom choosing to go into deep water where he has to use his wings in diving.

But during the winter when the streambanks are embossed in snow, and the streams themselves are chilled nearly to the freezing-point, so that the snow falling into them in stormy weather is not wholly dissolved, but forms a thin, blue sludge, thus rendering the current opaque—then he seeks the deeper portions of the main rivers, where he may dive to clear water beneath the sludge. Or he repairs to some open lake or millpond, at the bottom of which he feeds in safety.

When thus compelled to betake himself to a lake, he does not plunge into it at once like a duck, but always alights in the first place upon some rock or fallen pine along the shore. Then flying out thirty or forty yards, he alights with a dainty glint on the surface, swims about, looks down, finally makes up his mind, and disappears with a sharp stroke of his wings. After feeding for two or three minutes he suddenly reappears, showers the water from his wings with one vigorous shake, and rises abruptly into the air as if pushed up from beneath, comes back to his perch, sings a few minutes, and goes out to dive again; thus coming and going, singing and diving at the same place for hours.

The ouzel seldom swims more than a few yards on the surface, for, not being web-footed, he makes rather slow progress, but by means of his strong, crisp wings he swims, or rather flies, with celerity under the surface, often to considerable distances. But it is in withstanding the force of heavy rapids that his strength of wing in this respect is most strikingly manifested. One stormy morning in winter when the Merced River was blue and green with unmelted snow, I observed one of my ouzels perched on a snag out in the midst of a swift-rushing rapid, singing cheerily, as if everything was just to his mind; and while I stood on the bank admiring him, he suddenly plunged into the sludgy current, leaving his song abruptly broken off. After feeding a minute or two at the bottom, and when one would suppose that he must inevitably be swept far down-stream, he emerged just where he went down, alighted on the same snag, showered the water-beads from his feathers, and continued his unfinished song, seemingly in tranquil ease as if it had suffered no interruption.

—**John Muir**

Tundra Magic

Just east of the post was a wet meadow, almost a marsh, fringed with a sort of sedge that Sam called bog-cotton. Beyond this meadow a granite ridge half a mile long rose abruptly to a height of about thirty feet. From the post the ridge had a dark, colorless appearance. But when you examined the rocks carefully you found them to be covered with delicate lichens of many colors: gray-blue, pale green, orange-red, dusty yellow, and brown.

It was snowing lightly, now that it was September. The wind tossed the fragile flakes about playfully, tiring of them, letting them drop into the grass of the lowlands, into the clumps of willow, into the sheltered niches among the rocks. By evening there was a fluffy heap all along the base of the ridge and so much whiteness on the marsh that at a little distance you could not make out the waving white tassels of the bog-cotton.

I walked along the ridge, thinking of the winter. The wind had kept bare the most exposed places, and here the dry stems of the short weeds, the fine, curled grasses, and the cleft pods of legumes rustled and rattled.

I noted ahead of me a patch of snow, not as large as my hand, that, oddly enough, had defied the wind and clung to the very top of a rock. The mosses and epiphytes near this snow-patch were, perhaps, a little regular in pattern and there was a touch of red somewhere, not quite the red of a lichen or even a berry. Was there, near this patch of peculiar red, a bead of glistening black?

Hardly conscious that I had asked myself why patches of September snow should occasionally defy a strong wind, I walked closer . . . and a ptarmigan rose on neatly booted feet, craned his long neck, jerked his tail, and sauntered up the rock. The bead of glistening black was this ptarmigan's eye, the patch of red his naked brow!

How completely that bird had fooled me—not he himself, of course, for the ptarmigan probably didn't care whether I saw him or not—but that perfect color pattern of his! A patch of white winter plumage nestled among the grays and browns of his summer coat, just as the new snow-drift nestled between the base of the ridge and the brown marsh.

The ptarmigan was almost insolent. He walked out of the way merely to avoid having his tail trod upon. If in walking about him I took a course that promised him no physical discomfort, he remained motionless, eyeing me drowsily; or, to state the matter more accurately, including me in his looking simply because he was looking in my direction.

The ptarmigan was not, in fact, much interested in me.

My attitude toward the ptarmigan, on the other hand, was one of amazement. His plump form was neat in contour. The tiny vermilion comb above his eye set off the surrounding sombreness of moss and dry grass to perfection. His feet, feathered to the very claws, were lifted and set down upon the lichens with gentleness and unstudied precision. I marvelled that any single biological law, or complex set of laws, could account for a color pattern as handsome as that of his neck, back, and rump; and that, at precisely this season of the year, he should carry about on him his own little snowdrift, so that, whenever he chose, he could squat on the ground, begin to feel like any chance piece of old granite, look stonily at the world, in a manner of speaking, and all at once — well, simply cease to be a ptarmigan!

How fortunate, thought I, to come upon a ptarmigan so near the post! And a rock ptarmigan, too, the smaller and rarer of the two species found on Shugliak. What a sketch I would make — a sketch that would record that impertinent, lazy twinkle of eye, that reluctance to move one step out of the way, that plump squatness that might, without the remotest influence of any snake-haired Gorgon, on the instant turn to stone!

"Pe-ar, pee-ar!" came a gentle voice almost underfoot. There, about four feet away, its tail jerking half-acknowledgement of my presence, was another ptarmigan, another lichen-covered boulder with its little snowdrift. By the time I had crossed the ridge, bound for the salt-water "lake" beyond, I had encountered nine of the birds, apparently a family gathering of some sort, and I may not have met them all.

As I turned to leave the statuesque birds perched here and there on the rocks, I noticed, not far away, some feathers waving from a willow bush. Some of these proved to be patterned in gray, brown, and black; others were pure white. A white wing, its strong, curved, flight feathers stained with blood, lay to one side; to the bones clung bits of flesh, still damp. Here a ptarmigan, even he of the invisible cloak, had been struck to the ground by a gyrfalcon. He had moved at the wrong time. Tundra magic, this time, had failed. For there were eyes in this gray-brown world far sharper than mine.

— **George Miksch Sutton**

The rock ptarmigan has three plumages that blend with the arctic tundra: mottled brown and white like the snow-patched spring earth (left), gray in the fall like the rocks against which they nestle, and white like the winter landscape. Ptarmigans prefer high coastal barrens like those (above) on Canada's Baffin Island.

Flood Tide

The island lay in shadows only a little deeper than those that were swiftly stealing across the sound from the east. On its western shore the wet sand of the narrow beach caught the same reflection of palely gleaming sky that laid a bright path across the water from island beach to horizon. Both water and sand were the color of steel overlaid with the sheen of silver, so that it was hard to say where water ended and land began. . . .

With the dusk a strange bird came to the island from its nesting grounds on the outer banks. Its wings were pure black, and from tip to tip their spread was more than the length of a man's arm. It flew steadily and without haste across the sound, its progress as measured and as meaningful as that of the shadows which little by little were dulling the bright water path. The bird was called Rynchops, the black skimmer. . . .

About sunset the tide had been out. Now it was rising, covering the afternoon resting places of the skimmers, moving through the inlet, and flowing up into the marshes. Through most of the night the skimmers would feed, gliding on slender wings above the water in search of the small fishes that had moved in with the tide to the shelter of grassy shallows. Because they fed on the rising tide, the skimmers were called flood gulls.

On the south beach of the island, where water no deeper than a man's hand ran over gently ribbed bottom, Rynchops began to wheel and quarter over the shallows. He flew with a curious, lilting motion, lifting his wings high after the downstroke. His head was bent sharply so that the long lower bill, shaped like a scissor blade, might cut the water.

The blade or cutwater plowed a miniature furrow over the placid sheet of the sound, setting up wavelets of its own and sending vibrations thudding down through the water to rebound from the sandy bottom. The wave messages were received by the blennies and killifish that were roving the shallows on the alert for food. In the fish world many things are told by sound waves. Sometimes the vibrations tell of food animals like small shrimps or oar-footed crustaceans moving in swarms overhead. And so at the passing of the skimmer the small fishes came nosing at the surface, curious and hungry. Rynchops, wheeling about, returned along the way he had come and snapped up three of the fishes by the rapid opening and closing of his short upper bill. . . .

Rynchops swerved out around the dock that had been built by the fisherman who lived on the island, crossed the gutter, and swept far over the salt marshes, taking joy in flight and soaring motion. There he joined a flock of other skimmers and together they moved over the marshes in long lines and columns, sometimes appearing as dark shadows on the night sky; sometimes as spectral birds when, wheeling swallowlike in air, they showed white breasts and gleaming underparts. As they flew they raised their voices in the weird night chorus of the skimmers, a strange medley of notes high-pitched and low, now soft as the cooing of a mourning dove, and again harsh as the cawing of a crow; the whole chorus rising and falling, swelling and throbbing, dying away in the still air.

The flood gulls circled the island and crossed and recrossed the flats to the southward. All through the hours of the rising tide, they would hunt in flocks over the quiet waters of the sound. The skimmers loved nights of darkness and tonight thick clouds lay between the water and the moon's light.

Rachel Carson

With graceful precision, two black skimmers (above) plow the water with their lower beaks, creating a turbulence that attracts fish to the surface. The birds then retrace their flight path, scooping up the unwary fish whose curiosity has led them to their fate. Having eaten its fill, a skimmer returns to its nest on the open sand (far left) to incubate the eggs while its mate goes off to look for food. Skimmer chicks (near left) are hard to see because of their protective buff coloring and habit of crouching low in the sand. They leave the nest as soon as they are hatched.

63

Stranger than Fiction

Topsy-turvy flyers Hummingbirds are perhaps the best-known birds that can fly backwards; but herons and some other species have been known to flutter backwards briefly. During courtship, eagles, hawks, and ravens have been known to fly upside down.

Gizzards are tough. Some birds' gizzards, their millstone-like muscular stomachs used for grinding, are tough enough to bend steel needles or even crush hickory nuts—feats requiring anywhere from 125 to more than 300 pounds of pressure per square inch.

Weighty matters Cormorants and jackass penguins, which feed on fish, are said to swallow stones to make it easier to dive when fishing in salt water.

If it looks like an egg, hatch it! Black-crowned night herons have been seen trying to hatch toy blocks, and a bald eagle once spent weeks incubating a white rubber ball. One black-headed gull even tried to hatch an empty gun cartridge.

The bird that sews The tailorbird is just that, a tailor. To make its nest, it gathers leaves, punches holes along the edges, and sews them together with threads taken from spider webs, cocoons, or even sewing baskets.

If the nest fits . . . Nests of the penduline tits are so warm and snuggly that some European children actually use them for slippers.

Hard labor Kiwis have the toughest job when it comes to laying eggs. These chicken-sized New Zealand birds produce eggs ten times the size of hens' eggs—an effort that kills some of the flightless creatures.

The big mouth The sword-billed hummingbird of the Andes is almost all mouth; its five-inch bill is longer than the rest of its body.

Tyrants of the sky The tyrant flycatcher family certainly deserves its pugnacious name. Many of these spunky, robin-sized birds, which range from Argentina to the Arctic, will take on hawks or even eagles that invade their territories.

Heavy construction Whatever the reason, one crow must have been hard pressed for building material when it made its nest out of barbed wire. The same must have been true for the pigeon that used six-inch nails, plus a few feathers.

Some birds never seem to get their fill. Although hawks may feed their young about once an hour, and hummingbirds feed once in 20 minutes, one chickadee family was seen carrying food to the nest 35 times in 30 minutes—and a house wren family more than 1,200 times over a 15-hour period.

The flying sponge Adult desert sandgrouse may fly from two to forty miles for a drink. But what of the young, back at the nest? The father soaks his feathers at the water hole and later lets his youngsters draw out the water as if sucking on a wet cloth.

Working together African honeyguides get their name from their practice of guiding natives to nests with honey. After the honey is removed, the birds can get at what they were really after—the wax, which their unique metabolic system can digest.

What's in a name? America's English sparrow isn't a sparrow—and it isn't English. It's a member of the weaver finch family, common to all of Europe.

Rum runners Eggshells from the now-extinct elephant bird, _Aepyornis,_ were once used in Madagascar to carry rum—more than two gallons at a clip, in fact. These record-breaking shells would hold as many as 148 hen's eggs or 30,000 hummingbird's eggs.

Grub stake Lacking refrigerators, shrikes have their own bizarre but useful way of storing food: they impale their prey—insects, small rodents and lizards—on thorns until needed.

The entertainers Baya weaver birds in India have been trained to entertain audiences by using needles to thread beads onto cords.

The lonely vigil At brooding time, it's the male emperor penguin who incubates the egg—maintaining a lonely two-month vigil and never eating, losing up to 50 pounds, about half his total weight.

An egg a day—almost The champion egg layer is a domestic black Orpington of New Zealand, with a record 361 eggs in 364 days.

Hearty appetites When it comes to eating, Baltimore orioles certainly hold their own, downing as many as 17 hairy caterpillars a minute. Brown thrashers are no slackers either, capable of eating 6,000 insects in one day.

Eggs that roll in circles Murres, nesting on narrow ledges along steep cliffs, could be in danger of losing their eggs but for this factor: the eggs are tapered so sharply that when they edge toward the abyss, their shape lets them roll around safely in circles.

The parasites American cowbirds and European cuckoos lay their eggs in other species' nests, often discarding eggs to make room for their own. Most new parents, such as the hedge sparrow at right perched atop the young cuckoo it is feeding, seem to take no notice of the switch. ▶

In the Service of Man

Chickens, Chickens, Chickens

*"The partnership between chicken and man probably first began...
more than four thousand years ago."*

What is the most numerous bird in the world? Is it the starling or the grackle, which sometimes gather in flocks of several hundred thousands and make themselves into a local disaster? Is it the sea gull, which haunts coastlines and garbage dumps around the world? No. It is the domestic chicken. There are more chickens in the world than human beings, and there are billions of us. The United States alone has a chicken population of about 2.3 *billion*. And there are millions more chickens in other parts of the world, for chickens are raised on every continent except Antarctica. Chickens supply eggs, meat, and other valuable products, and raising chickens is a multi-billion-dollar business.

The partnership between chicken and man probably first began in northwest India more than four thousand years ago. And it *is* a partnership, though an unequal one. While man kills chickens for food and takes their eggs, he also feeds them, shelters them, and gives them protection against predators.

Man must have hunted the wild jungle fowl for centuries before he finally thought of capturing some of these tasty birds and raising them. But judging from evidence found among the ruins of ancient cities in India, man did not eat his tamed jungle fowl. Instead, he used them in religious ceremonies dedicated to the sun. Jungle fowl, like their tame descendants, wake up at sunrise, and the males greet the sun with loud crowing. Modern ethologists (scientists who study animal behavior) believe that a cock crows to tell his rivals: "Here I am! This is my territory! Stay off!" But primitive man thought the birds were calling out to the sun-god, their protector.

The sacred chickens of ancient India were probably sacrificed to the sun-god. In a mystical way, each god was supposed to enjoy the spiritual essence of the animals that were killed for him. The priests then ate the earthly remains that were left.

The cocks were probably also pitted against each other in ritual combat as a kind of fertility magic. In the wild, male jungle fowl duel each other at mating time. By restaging these duels with captive jungle fowl, primitive man believed he could magically create fertility. The people would have many children to work in the fields, the animals would grow fat and increase their numbers, and the crops would bear bountifully.

Fed and protected by man, the sacred fowl multiplied. There were more birds than the priests needed for their rituals. Sooner or later, common people must have begun keeping the surplus chickens for their own use, eating the eggs and sometimes the birds themselves. Around

1000 B.C., religious laws of northwestern India forbade the eating of chickens, which is a pretty strong clue that people were doing it.

Chickens seem to have spread fairly quickly throughout most of eastern Asia. But they were much slower in reaching the West. Trading vessels brought chickens to Egypt around 1300 B.C., but the birds disappeared and didn't turn up there again until about 300 B.C.—a lapse of a thousand years. Still, chicken keeping did spread westward. It reached Persia about 1000 B.C., and from Persia chickens spread to the neighboring region of Mesopotamia.

Gradually, the people around the eastern end of the Mediterranean Sea learned about chicken keeping from their neighbors. The Greeks knew about chickens (which they called "Persian birds") as early as 800 B.C., and chickens were common throughout the Greek lands by 500 B.C. (about the time the Roman Republic was being founded). The Greeks at first raised chickens mainly for the "sport" of cockfighting, which by then had become a bloodthirsty popular amusement. They also raised chickens to sacrifice to their many unpredictable gods. Eventually, the Greeks too made chickens part of their ordinary farm livestock.

The Romans probably acquired chickens from Greek colonists who had settled in Italy. The Romans used chickens in foretelling the future. Before any important state event, specially trained experts called *haruspices* would kill some of the sacred chickens from the temple of Jupiter and inspect their livers. From the shape and color of the unfortunate fowls' livers, they would attempt to predict the fate decreed by the gods.

A less wasteful way of making prophecies was to place an offering of grain before the sacred chickens. If the birds ate heartily, it meant success; if they pecked listlessly at their food or ignored it, failure was the message of the gods. This kind of chicken prophecy was used especially to foretell the outcome of battles.

The Greeks bred fighting cocks on a semiscientific basis, selecting them for the most desirable qualities. But the Romans were the first to breed chickens systematically as a source of food. Roman writers gave great attention to the design of hen houses and the need for keeping them clean. The Romans may also have been the

Charles Darwin identified the red jungle fowl (left) of northern India as the progenitor of the domestic chicken (overleaf). By 2500 B.C., the people of this region kept tame fowl but were prohibited by law from eating them because of their importance in prophecy and religion.

first people to fumigate chicken houses against insect pests. For this, they used the choking fumes of burning sulfur and pitch.

Throughout ancient times farm chickens were raised chiefly for eggs. Hens were eaten only when they were too old to lay any more. If they were tough and stringy, no one cared. The quality of peasants' food was not high in any case. The cockerels (young male birds), however, were killed when young and plump and sold as a delicacy.

Unlike the peasants, wealthy Romans were very particular about what they ate. They demanded that their chickens be specially fattened for the table. One way of doing this was to tie the chickens down and force-feed them with grain through a funnel. The Romans also practiced the art of caponizing—that is, castrating young cockerels. Deprived of their male hormones, these birds grew soft and plump without any special fattening.

While Roman gourmets and poultry raisers were developing these refinements, the rugged Roman legions carried live chickens as provisions for the officers and crew. The Pilgrims acquired chickens after they had settled in permanently. As European settlements spread in North America, chickens became an important part of the household. Following the old European custom, the chickens belonged to the chief woman of the family. The eggs and fowls were her main source of private income. Sometimes a farm wife was expected to keep her children clothed with the proceeds from her flock of chickens until the children went to school. Not only farm families had chickens; even city dwellers kept a few hens in the backyard, feeding them on table scraps.

The Colonial chickens were of the common barnyard type—of no particular breed. In fact, until the 1800s no one paid much attention to the particular breed of chicken as long as the chickens laid eggs now and then. But in the early 1800s scientific farming began to take hold in the United States, and part of scientific farming was developing pure breeds of animals.

Farmers began to keep records of the bloodlines of

were conquering all the lands around the Mediterranean, plus big chunks of western and central Europe. Wherever the legions went, chickens followed. By the time the Roman Empire collapsed during the fifth century A.D., chickens were firmly established in most of Europe, North Africa, and Asia. But chickens did not reach the Negro peoples who lived south of the Sahara until many centuries later, for the Sahara was too formidable a barrier to transport livestock across. The Spaniards brought chickens to the New World, and English, French, and Dutch colonists soon brought their own familiar breeds. A few centuries before, Polynesian voyagers had brought chickens to the far-flung islands of the Pacific.

The Pilgrims who came to New England on the *Mayflower* did not bring chickens with them, for the ship was too crowded, although ships at that time sometimes their stock—even their chickens—and to establish standards of appearance for the animals. As new strains of chickens appeared, societies were formed for the advancement of the breed. Yearly contests for the best of the breed were held. Chickens that failed to meet the standards for size, shape, color of feathers, shape of comb, and so on were removed from the flocks. The competitions encouraged farmers to keep records of egg and meat production and to breed those chickens that performed best, resulting in our modern breeds that lay an average of 238 eggs per hen each year.

— **Peter R. Limburg**

Man has altered both the genes and the life style of chickens. Bred for egg production, layer hens (above) spend their lives in wire cages. Bred for beauty, some prize specimens of Japanese long-tailed fowl (right) are prohibited from mating lest they damage their splendid feathers.

Hung, Strung, and Potted

Chickens are believed to have been introduced into the colonies at Jamestown about 1607, and by 1700 were so plentiful that they were no longer recorded on inventories of family property.

Most chickens were simply roasted, but a more festive dish was chicken fricasseed in rich brown gravy with wild herbs. The forerunner of modern fried poultry was a concoction named pulled chicken, which involved jerking large chunks of raw meat from the bird's bones and browning the morsels in deep fat.

Eggs from chickens and other fowl such as wild plovers were eaten by all economic classes, but were usually not served at breakfast time. Most colonists preferred their eggs either poached, stewed, battered, or fried, and then served as a side dish at dinner or supper.

Peacocks, imported into Jamestown at the same time as chickens, were bred less successfully for food, and a later attempt to introduce pheasants and partridges into the colonies also failed. The experiment, conducted on a New Jersey estate owned by Benjamin Franklin's son-in-law, Richard Bache, was halted when the entire pheasant flock failed to survive the first year's winter. Within several years after the country's settlement, however, geese and ducks became domesticated and large backyard flocks provided settlers with poultry on a year-round basis.

Falcons, hawks, eagles, and buzzards, though never domesticated, were hunted widely as food sources, as was almost any type of songbird. Near the sea and on inland rivers, wild waterfowl were plentiful everywhere during most seasons, with teals, cranes, herons, swans, geese, and ducks frequently roasted or stewed into soup.

Wild birds were prepared much like chicken, but with a shorter cooking time. Recipes ranged from a simple roasted bird to an elaborate potted fowl, which was preserved in containers of highly flavored gelatin. In addition to providing settlers with an abundant supply of foodstuffs, wildfowl were also indispensable as a source of household necessities such as down for mattresses and quills for writing pens.

Colonial terminology for the carving of fowl was considerably more complicated than today. In prerevolutionary times, specific names were given to the slicing of each type of bird. A swan was "lifted"; a goose "broken"; hens were "spoiled"; a mallard "unbraced"; pigeons were "winged"; and woodcocks "thighed."

Turkeys were plentiful throughout the year and their importance as a food can scarcely be overemphasized. Size estimates of wild turkeys ranged up to fifty pounds, but like the deer, this bird's abundance quickly diminished. One reason was extensive hunting by colonists. Another factor in the decline was the practice of early settlers to gather the wild ginseng berry, a favorite turkey food. Unlike most other berries, ginseng was not eaten locally, but the plant and roots were exported profitably to the Chinese drug market where it was processed into a medicinal narcotic.

Successful efforts were made to maintain the distinctive flavor of the wild turkey. Early housewives hunted eggs in the forests and the young chicks were later bred to domestic strains, thus producing a cross match of flavors.

Ironically, the passenger pigeon, probably the most widely eaten bird in colonial times, is now extinct. For many centuries, North American Indians valued this most numerous of all fowls, not only for its sweet flesh, but for its oil, which was used in cooking. One Indian village of seventeen families is recorded as having in storage at least one hundred gallons of the bird oil.

Early cookbooks are filled with scores of recipes for preparing passenger pigeons in every conceivable manner. The birds were stewed, fricasseed, fried, boiled, roasted, hashed, cooked into pies, and preserved. But for the present-day cook, these formulas are simply reminders of an animal who has passed from the scene. Martha, the last of the passenger pigeons, died on September 1, 1914, at the Cincinnati Zoological Park.

Another fowl that failed to survive the settler's hunting techniques was the heath hen. This grouse-type bird was also numerous during the colonial era, but decreased rapidly in numbers during the nineteenth century. Servants in Boston are recorded as protesting that their meals were too dependent upon the heath hen and demanded more variety. But like the passenger pigeon, attempts to save the few remaining hens were unsuccessful and it too was erased from the records of living species. The heath hen's final refuge was on Martha's Vineyard.

Quail, grouse, woodcock, plover, curlew, and even larks were eaten by American pioneers, but unlike the passenger pigeon and the heath hen, their numbers increased. As more and more dense forests were cleared and fields planted in grain, flocks of these birds rapidly multiplied and their descendants are with us today.

Many of the birds hunted for colonial cooking pots are now protected by federal migratory laws and vigorously enforced state statutes. Thus, today's cooks may never have the opportunity of sampling roasted robin or bobolink stew. But recipes for fowl such as chicken and turkey, together with legally hunted game birds, can be re-created as deliciously today as they were hundreds of years ago.

— **Sally Smith Booth**

Recipes from the Past

To Stew Pigeons

Stuff the birds with seasoning made of ground pepper, salt, mace and sweet herbs. Half roast them, then put them in a stew pan with a sufficient quantity of gravy, a little white wine, some pickled mushrooms and lemon peel. When stewed enough, take out the birds, thicken the liquor with butter and the yolks of eggs.

The New England Cookery, 1808

To Roast Widgeon, Duck, Teal or Moorhen

The flavor is best preserved without stuffing; but put some pepper, salt and a bit of butter in the birds. Wild fowl require to be much less done than tame, and to be served of a fine color.

The basting ordered takes off the fishy taste which wild fowl sometimes have. Send up a very good gravy in the dish; and on cutting the breast, half a lemon squeezed over, with pepper on it improves the taste.

Or stuff them with crumbs, a little shred onion, sage, pepper and salt, but not a large quantity, and add a bit of butter. Slice an onion, and put into the dripping pan, with a little salt, and baste the fowls with it till three parts done: then remove that, and baste with butter. They should come up finely frothed, and not be overdone.

A New System of Domestic Cookery, 1807

To Fricassee Chicken

Cut up the chickens raw, in the manner as you do for eating, and flat the pieces a little with a rolling pin. Fry them of a light brown; afterwards put them into a stew pan, with sufficient quantity but not too much gravy, a spoonful or two of white wine, to two or three chickens, a little nutmeg and salt. Thicken it with flour and butter. Garnish with sippets within the dish, and with crisp parsley on the rim.

The Frugal Housewife, 1772

To Stuff a Turkey

Grate a wheat loaf, one quarter of a pound of butter, one quarter of a pound of salt pork, finely chopped, two eggs, a little sweet marjoram, summer savory, parsley, pepper and salt (If the pork be not sufficiently) fill the bird and sew it up. The same will answer for all wild fowl. Water fowls require onions. The same ingredients stuff a leg of veal, fresh pork, or a loin of veal.

New American Cookery, 1805

The Pilgrim settlers of Plymouth, Massachusetts, set abundant tables like the one shown here at Harlow House, a restored colonial dwelling.

Grouse Feathers

My intimate association with grouse has extended over a period of nearly forty years. In that time I have come to regard him as the wisest and, also, the most foolish of birds. His keenness of sight and hearing is a thing to marvel at. His knowledge as to the psychological moment for bursting into sudden, startled and startling flight is a thing which he has acquired from countless ancestors.

Through what process of instinct or reason this glorious bird has come to realize that only through invisibility, even while on the wing, is he safe, is a thing to ponder over. He knows it, however, and he knows it thoroughly. Hundreds of times I have caught grouse in positions where they had to fly a number of feet to gain cover. That cover might be the bole of a single big tree, or perhaps an evergreen but a few feet high. It has been a delight to see the bird explode (that word seems to best describe the action) into instantaneous, full speed in the direction of that bit of protecting cover. Oftentimes, to reach it, he must fly nearer to me than when he started.

Many times he comes so near that I, involuntarily, dodge to give him room to pass. His bright, shoe-button eye peers up at me as he hurtles past and he whistles a soft little "quit-quit-quit." A split second before he reaches that bit of cover he banks sharply, with a tilt of his wide-spreading tail, and slides in behind that sheltering screen. As he disappears from view his head is still turned. One beady eye watches me while the other charts the course ahead as he glides, swiftly out of gunshot.

He will sit as immovable as a stone while you tramp past him within a score of feet. Then, when you have stepped behind a bush, he will hammer out behind you, causing you to turn completely about, a physical contortion which is not conducive of steady shooting.

He will perch on the branch of a tree and peer down at you while you pretend not to see him and tramp, sturdily, past until you have reached that spot you have in mind where it will be necessary for him to give you a fairly open shot.

Then, when you slip the safety off the gun, and turning, say, "All right, old fellow. Do your stuff," he perversely refuses to fly. After a moment you look down for a stick or stone to toss at him, and—"Whirr-r-r!" he is gone—over your head, directly back through the tree, or hardest of all, in a rushing sweep down to within a few inches of the ground.

He will run ahead of your dog from one cover to the next, for hundreds of yards, until he tires of the game, whereupon he will run through a tangle of foliage and

*"The moment the dog winded him that old cock
would start running. . . . He would travel fast, and
the moment he came to the clearing beyond the pine
growth he would take wing. I could hear the thunder
of his take-off while I was still fifty yards away."*

"HUNTING THE EDGES" BY ROBERT ABBETT, 1978.

flush instantly when he reaches the clearing beyond.

I remember one wise old cock who fooled me for several years so nicely, so smoothly, and so consistently that the hunting of him became a sort of rite with me; a rite which I religiously performed several times each fall, until, through no fault of mine, we drifted apart. During those years I learned, firstly, to respect him for his superior woodsmanship and then, later, to like him for himself alone. The last two years my affection for the old fellow was genuine, and although I tried every trick I knew to get one close, open shot at him during that period, I vowed that, should I ever do so, I would not pull the trigger.

He was distrustful of me, and rightly so, for I treated him shamefully on our first meeting. It was my first trip to a glorious cover so remote and inaccessible that only a few of the incurables hunt it.

On that day, I had just entered the woods when the dog came to a staunch point. By his bulging eyes I judged the bird was close by, so I stepped directly in front of him. A woodcock arose almost at my feet and bounced up toward the tree tops. It was an easy shot, and I killed her, broke the gun, tossed away the empty shell, and was reaching for a fresh one when a magnificent cock grouse hammered up through the trees before me.

That is always an awkward position to be in when a bird flushes. Part of a precious second is lost in trying to decide which is the quicker, to thrust the fresh shell into the empty chamber or to drop it back in the pocket, close the gun and shoot the other barrel. I chose the latter course, snapped the gun to my shoulder, and shot, but I knew, while pulling the trigger, I was too slow. He had gained his coveted shelter ere the shot splashed in behind him, and I saw him no more that fall. The next year there was a tremendously big cock in that bit of woods. He was an old bird and a wary one, and I had a feeling it was the same grouse I had shot at the previous fall. He had matriculated in the school of experience, and made the dog and me look foolish.

There was a flock of young birds there, too, and they were unusually shy for such a remote covert. I visited the place several times that season and found the old fellow waiting for me each time. The moment the dog winded him that old cock would start running, along a hardwood ridge, down through a little valley, up a bank, and through a patch of pines. He would travel fast, and the moment he came to the clearing beyond the pine growth he would take wing. I could hear the thunder of his take-off while I was still fifty yards away.

Beyond thinking that here was a particularly shy old grouse, I gave the matter no serious consideration until the same thing had happened several times. Then it gradually dawned on me that here was a bird who was having a quiet laugh at my expense, and I decided to match my wits against his.

Accordingly I took a boy with me, and when we reached the covert, put the dog on leash and gave the youth orders to release and follow the dog in ten minutes. Then, by a roundabout course I made my way to the clearing beyond the pines where the old fellow took to the air, took my stand on a big stump just back of the stone wall that marked the boundary of that bit of pine growth, and waited to see what would happen. In a few minutes I heard the tinkle of the bell on the dog and the crashing of brush under the hurrying feet of the boy. A moment later my very shy friend hopped on the stone wall some twenty yards before me. He spotted me instantly, and his head bobbed inquisitively as he looked me over.

"Come on," I invited. "See if you can make it across the clearing this time," whereupon he turned, dropped back on the further side of the wall, ran thirty yards back in the pines, almost directly toward the dog, and rocketed up through the trees and away for hundreds of yards up the steep mountain-side.

Several times each year for two years more I tried every trick I knew to outwit that wily old general. Several times I saw him running where I could have killed him, but never again, after that first time, did he make the mistake of getting into the air within forty yards of me.

When, in the fifth consecutive shooting season, I failed to start the old fellow, I felt a keen personal loss. I had grown to like him, and I am sure I would not have killed him then, had the chance occurred; but he had gone forever. I do not believe any other hunter killed him fairly. He may have been ambushed and slain, but I prefer to think otherwise. Far better the silent swoop of a giant owl in the blackness of a stormy night, or the ice sheet forming over the deep snows which were his winter bed, freezing over head, drop by drop, as they formed that glistening white pall from which there is no escape—the glistening pall of death.

I go back there once each year, but the woods seem somber and cheerless. The north wind sucks down through that giant pass in the hills and chills the marrow in my bones. The warmth and friendliness of the place are gone, and the hills seem steeper than in those other days. Can it be that I am growing old, or do I miss the

"Through what process of instinct or reason this glorious bird has come to realize that only through invisibility, even while on the wing, is he safe, is a thing to ponder over. He knows it, however, and he knows it thoroughly."

gay, bold spirit which made of self-confident, conceited me, and clever, bird-wise old Duke, a pair of the rankest of rank amateurs?

The wisdom of the ruffed grouse is unquestioned; yet it is always a source of wonder to me why he, with his college education, will do the many fool things he is guilty of.

A grouse will fly through trees and brush at full speed a hundred times, and never ruffle a feather; yet if you drive that same bird across an opening which contains a house or barn, it is not at all unusual for him to crash into it with all the reckless abandon of a drunken truck-driver attacking a railway train.

He will run ahead of your dog and flush out of range a half dozen times. Then at the next point he may sit beneath a bush, which he well knows is no protection, and insist on your kicking him before he will fly.

A grouse is extremely cautious and always apprehensive of danger, but as a rule he seems to have no pre-conceived plan of action. The relative position of his enemy and himself when his one-track mind prompts him to take flight seems to be the factor which determines his line of flight.

I remember one occasion when my shooting companion and I drove a flock of several grouse the length of a covert some five hundred yards long and nearly as wide. They were wild, and flushed ahead of the dog beyond shooting range. Straight ahead they went, all rising at once, and we followed, knowing their last flight would carry them to the edge of the wood. Beyond lay an open field, and it seemed quite certain they would lie well to the dog ere they broke across the clearing or back over our heads.

The dog worked ahead and pointed where we knew the birds would be, and we grinned knowingly at each other, pulled our sleeves up and worked in, prepared for a few glorious moments of intense action.

Again they went up, well out of gunshot, and across the open field. A hundred yards out in that field was a little depression some fifty feet across, and in it grew a matted tangle of high-bushed blueberries. There was no other cover near, and we knew that no grouse with a molecule of brains would stop in a place like that—but every last bird dropped into that little patch of bushes.

Now here, we told ourselves, was a chance such as seldom came to grouse hunters. We would separate, and come down on them in such a manner that no matter which way they went, one of us would be within range.

We did that, making a wide detour, and came down on that little patch of bushes from opposite sides. We were within range now, thirty yards—twenty—ten. The dog was pointing staunchly on the windward side. We had made no mistake, the grouse were there—but why didn't they get up? We advanced the few remaining steps to the edge of the bushes, and still not a bird moved.

I kicked a bush, and instantly we could hear them whistling that soft little "quit-quit-quit" of alarm.

"Watch out! I'm going to throw a rock in there."

"O.K. Let'er go."

Crash! Thr-r-r-up! A lone grouse hammered up head-high, spotted us instantly, and dropped into the bush.

"They're over on this side now. Watch out. I'll throw this stick in there."

Whish-sh! Thr-r-r-up! Exactly the same as before.

"Send the dog in and let him put them up."

"Send him in yourself—if you think you can. He'll point there until we are gray headed if the birds lie. He's staunch, that dog."

"Great chance for a double, or a pair of them, if we can only get them up."

"I've hunted pa'tridge for twenty years and I'll be damned if I ever saw anything like this. Five minutes ago they were as wild as a bunch of chorus girls, and now you couldn't make them fly with a charge of dynamite."

"Let's work in a little way together, and don't shoot at singles. That would be too easy. Let's see if a pair will put up together."

We took a few cautious steps into the brush and "Whir-r-r—Whir-r-r;" a pair got up simultaneously and started for the woods. I swung on the left hand bird and pulled the trigger. "Crack!" Both birds collapsed and dropped dead in the open field.

We backed out, cautiously, and gathered up the birds. The dog was still frozen, motionless, on point. We looked at him, and then at each other.

"What do you say?" I asked. "Shall we try it again?"

"Hell, no," he said, in the mild, expressionless manner which is his custom. "That's premeditated murder. Let 'em live."

We left them there, but we went back again, a week later. That day was one of the many I shall never forget. More birds had come into the covert and they lay perfectly for the dog. We were in top form, that day, and took the limit with hardly a miss, and departed with the comfortable assurance that there were more than enough birds remaining for breeders the next year.

Burton L. Spiller

Fishing With Feathered Lightning

...a flock of trained cormorants would have put a well-trained pack of foxhounds to shame. Once they'd located a school of fish, they'd ... form a ring around it. Then they'd work inward, grabbing fish as they went."

Fishing with cormorants is an ancient sport; records of it go back to 1000 BC and it was probably old then. Some ingenious individual noticed that in streams and lakes where it was impractical to use nets, the cormorants seemed to be doing fine, and he conceived the idea of training cormorants to fish with collars around their necks so they couldn't swallow their catch. The Chinese made quite an art out of the business. They wouldn't use wild birds but developed their own breed of cormorants, raising the birds in big hatcheries like chickens. Friar Odoric, a 14th-century missionary, called them "water crows" which the French translated as *corbeaux marins.* Hence our word "cormorant."

When the young birds could swim, they were tethered near the edge of a lake on long strings, and small dead fish were thrown into the shallow water. As the fish were thrown, the trainer whistled the "dive" call. When each bird had got its fish, it was pulled out by the string while the trainer whistled the "retrieve" signal. Then the bird was rewarded.

According to accounts, a flock of trained cormorants would have put a well-trained pack of foxhounds to shame. Once they'd located a school of fish, they'd spread out and form a ring around it. Then they'd work inward, grabbing fish as they went. When one bird swam back to the boat to disgorge its catch, the two cormorants on either side closed in to take its place. If one bird got out of line, the whole flock would scream and beat with their wings until the miscreant got back in formation. Friar Odoric claims the birds would even disgorge the fish themselves without any help from the fisherman, each bird putting its catch into its own basket. There was always a head cormorant which acted as a kind of top sergeant, and the Japanese called this bird *Ichi* ("the

"CORMORANT FISHING ON THE NAGARA RIVER" BY KEISAI EISEN (1792-1848). OPPOSITE: "CORMORANT" BY MIYAMOTO NITEN (1584-1645).

boss"). If any of the other birds misbehaved, Ichi beat it up. Ichi always sat on the boat's bow and the rest were lined up according to rank.

Modern Japanese cormorant fishing is a long way from this highly skilled business. It is done at night with a brazier full of live coals on the boat's bow to attract fish. The cormorants are never at liberty; each is controlled by a long string, and is dragged back to the boat after making a catch. Here the fisherman chokes it until it coughs up the fish. One fisherman can handle the strings of a dozen birds without getting himself and the cormorants tied into a bowknot. No longer done commercially, it is kept up only as a tourist attraction.

Cormorant fishing as a sport was introduced into Europe by the Dutch in the 16th century. It caught on rapidly as a sort of underwater falconry, the birds being allowed complete freedom and trained to come on com-

mand. Henry IV of France practiced it, and Louis XIII had a series of canals built at Fontainebleau for it.

During the early part of this century, cormorant fishing was revived in France. The Count de Najac took the sport so seriously that he dressed as a Chinese mandarin to practice it. And cormorant fishing nearly caused a diplomatic breach between France and Italy. Napoleon III described the sport to the Italian monarch, but he called the birds "pelicans." Delighted with the idea, the king summoned his head keeper (whose experience with birds had been limited to pheasants) and ordered him to train a flock of pelicans. After months of hard work, the poor fellow gave up and told His Majesty Napoleon must have been fooling him. The king wrote Napoleon in a rage and much diplomatic maneuvering was required to soothe royal feelings.

———————————————— **Dan Mannix** 79

The Goshawk

*"A goshawk...was
not meant to run away
but to run after."*

When I first saw him he was a round thing like a clothes basket covered with sacking. But he was tumultuous and frightening, repulsive in the same way as snakes are frightening to people who do not know them, or dangerous as the sudden movement of a toad by the door step when one goes out at night with a lantern into the dew. The sacking had been sewn with string, and he was bumping against it from underneath: bump, bump, bump, incessantly, with more than a hint of lunacy. The basket pulsed like a big heart in fever. It gave out weird cries of protest, hysterical, terrified, but furious and authoritative. It would have eaten anybody alive.

Imagine what his life had been till then. When he was an infant, still unable to fly and untidy with bits of fluff, still that kind of mottled, motive and gaping toad which confronts us when we look into birds' nests in May: when, moreover, he was a citizen of Germany, so far away: a glaring man had come to his mother's nest with a basket like this one, and had stuffed him in. He had never seen a human being, never been confined in such a box, which smelled of darkness and manufacture and the stink of man. It must have been like death—the thing which we can never know beforehand—as, with clumsy talons groping for an unnatural foothold, his fledgeling consciousness was hunched and bundled in the oblong, alien surroundingness. The guttural voices, the unbird-like den he was taken to, the scaly hands which bound him, the second basket, the smell and noise of the motor car, the unbearable, measured clamour of the aircraft which bounced those skidding talons on the untrustworthy woven floor all the way to England: heat, fear, noise, hunger, the reverse of nature: with these to stomach, terrified, but still nobly and madly defiant, the eyas goshawk had arrived at my small cottage in his accursed basket—a wild and adolescent creature whose father and mother in eagles' nests had fed him with bloody meat still quivering with life, a foreigner from far black pine slopes, where a bundle of precipitous sticks and some white droppings, with a few bones and feathers splashed over the tree foot, had been to him the ancestral heritage. He was born to fly, sloping sideways, free among the verdure of that Teutonic upland, to murder with his fierce feet and to consume with that curved Persian beak, who now hopped up and down in the clothes basket with a kind of imperious precocity, the impatience of a spoiled but noble heir apparent to the Holy Roman Empire.

I picked up the clothes basket in a gingerly way and carried it to the barn. The workman's cottage which I lived in had been built under Queen Victoria, with barn and pigsty and bakehouse, and it had once been inhabited by a gamekeeper. There in the wood, long ago when Englishmen lived their own sports, instead of competing at games with tedious abstract tennis bats and cricket sticks as they do today, the keeper who lived in the cottage had reared his pheasants. There was no wire netting in his days, and the windows of the low barn were enclosed with wooden slats, nailed criss-cross, a diamond lattice work. I put Gos down in the barn, in his basket, and was splitting a rabbit's head to get at the brain, when two friends whose sad employment I had lately followed came to take me to a public house for the last time. The hawk came out of the basket already strong on the wing, beat up to the rafters, while his master, armed with two pairs of leather gloves on each hand, cowered near the floor—and then there was no more time. I had intended to put a pair of jesses on him at once, but he flew up before I had pulled myself together: and it was only when the great bundle of young feathers was perching on the rafters that one could see the jesses already on him. Jesses were what they called the thongs about his feet. Jessed but not belled, perched at the top of the old gamekeeper's loft, baleful and extraordinary, I left the goshawk to settle down: while we three went out to the public house for a kind of last supper, at which none was more impatient of translation than the departing guest.

They brought me back at about eleven o'clock, and by midnight I had given them drink and wished them fortune. They were good people, . . . but I was glad . . . to turn to the cobwebby outhouse where Gos and a new destiny sat together in contrary arrogance.

The hawk was on the highest rafter, out of reach, looking down with his head on one side and a faint suggestion of Lars Porsena. Humanity could not get there.

Fortunately my human manoeuvres disturbed the creature, shook him off the high perch to which he was entitled by nature and unused by practice—unused by the practice which had stormed at him with mechanical noises and shaken him with industrial jolts and bent his tail feathers into a parody of a Woolworth mop.

He flew, stupid with too many experiences, off the perch at which he would have been impregnable. There was sorrow in the inapt evasion. A goshawk, too gigantic for a British species, and only three inches shorter than the golden eagle, was not meant to run away but to run after. The result was that now in this confinement of unknown brick walls, he fled gauchely, round and about

> *"...the Boke of St. Albans had laid down*
> *precisely the classes of people to whom any proper-*
> *minded member of the Falconidae might belong.*
> *...Well, a goshawk was the proper servant for a*
> *yeoman, and I was well content with that."*

FALCONER IN WEST PAKISTAN·

the dreary room: until he was caught after a few circuits by the jesses, and I stood, stupefied at such temerity, with the monster on my fist.

The yellowish breast-feathers—Naples Yellow—were streaked downward with long, arrow-shaped hackles of Burnt Umber: his talons, like scimitars, clutched the leather glove on which he stood with a convulsive grip: for an instant he stared upon me with a mad, marigold or dandelion eye, all his plumage flat to the body and his head crouched like a snake's in fear or hatred, then bated wildly from the fist.

Bated. They still said that Jones minor got into a bate that morning, at preparatory schools. It was a word that had been used since falcons were first flown in England, since England was first a country therefore. It meant the headlong dive of rage and terror, by which a leashed hawk leaps from the fist in a wild bid for freedom, and hangs upside down by his jesses in a flurry of pinions like a chicken being decapitated, revolving, struggling, in danger of damaging his primaries.

It was the falconer's duty to lift the hawk back to the fist with his other hand in gentleness and patience, only to have him bate again, once, twice, twenty, fifty times, all night—in the shadowy, midnight barn, by the light of the second-hand paraffin lamp.

It was two years ago [In 1937]. I had never trained a serious hawk before, nor met a living falconer, nor seen a hawk that had been trained. I had three books.

One of them was by Gilbert Blaine, the second was a half-volume in the Badminton Library and the third was Bert's *Treatise of Hawks and Hawking*, which had been printed in 1619. From these I had a theoretical idea, and a very out-of-date idea, of the way to man a hawk.

In teaching a hawk it was useless to bludgeon the creature into submission. The raptors had no tradition of masochism, and the more one menaced or tortured them, the more they menaced in return. Wild and intransigent, it was yet necessary to 'break' them some-how or other, before they could be tamed and taught. Any cruelty, being immediately resented, was worse than useless, because the bird would never bend or break to it. He possessed the last inviolable sanctuary of death. The mishandled raptor chose to die.

So the old hawk-masters had invented a means of taming them which offered no visible cruelty, and whose secret cruelty had to be born by the trainer as well as by the bird. They kept the bird awake. Not by nudging it, or by any mechanical means, but by walking about with their pupil on the fist and staying awake themselves. The hawk was 'watched,' was deprived of sleep by a sleep-less man, day and night, for a space of two, three or as much as nine nights together. It was only the stupid teachers who could go as far as nine nights: the genius could do with two, and the average man with three. All the time he treated his captive with more than every courtesy, more than every kindness and consideration. The captive did not know that it was being kept awake by an act of will, but only that it was awake, and in the end, becoming too sleepy to mind what happened, it would droop its head and wings and go to sleep on the fist. It would say: 'I am so tired that I will accept this curious perch, repose my trust in this curious creature, anything so I may rest.'

This was what I was now setting out to do. I was to stay awake if necessary for three days and nights, during which, I hoped, the tyrant would learn to stop his bating and to accept my hand as a perch, would consent to eat there and would become a little accustomed to the strange life of human beings.

In this there was much interest and joy—the joy of the discoverer—much to think about, and very much to observe. It meant walking round and round in the lamp-light, constantly lifting back the sufferer, with a gentle hand under his breast, after the hundredth bate: it meant humming to oneself untunefully, talking to the hawk, stroking his talons with a feather when he did consent to stay on the glove: it meant reciting Shakespeare to keep awake, and thinking with pride and happiness about the hawk's tradition.

Falconry was perhaps the oldest sport persisting in the world. There was a bas-relief of a Babylonian with a hawk on his fist in Khorsabad, which dated from 3000 years ago. Many people were not able to understand why this was pleasant, but it was. I thought it was right that I should now be happy to continue as one of a long line.

Hawks were the nobility of the air, ruled by the eagle. They were the only creatures for which man had troubled to legislate. We still passed laws which preserved certain birds or made certain ways of taking them illegal, but we never troubled to lay down rules for the birds themselves. We did not say that a pheasant must only belong to a civil servant or a partridge to an inspector-of-filling-up-forms. But in the old days, when to understand the manage of a falcon was the criterion by which a gentleman could be recognized—and in those days a gentleman was a defined term, so that to be proclaimed 'noe gent.' by a college of arms was equivalent to being proclaimed no airman by the Royal Aero Club or no motorist by the licensing authorities—the *Boke of St. Albans* had laid down precisely the classes of people to whom any properminded member of the Falconidae might belong. An eagle for an emperor, a peregrine for an earl: the list had defined itself meticulously downward to the kestrel, and he, as a crowning insult, was allowed to belong to a mere knave—because he was useless to be trained. Well, a goshawk was the proper servant for a yeoman, and I was well content with that.

There were two kinds of these raptors, the long- and the short-winged hawks. Long-winged hawks, whose first primary feather was the longest, were the 'falcons,' who were attended by falconers. Short-winged hawks, whose fourth primary was the longest, were the true 'hawks,' who were attended by austringers. Falcons flew high and stooped upon their quarry: hawks flew low, and slew by stealth. Gos was a chieftain among the latter.

But it was his own personality that gave more pleasure than his lineage. He had a way of looking. Cats can watch a mousehole cruelly, dogs can be seen to watch their masters with love, a mouse watched Robert Burns with fear. Gos watched intently. It was an alert, concentrated, piercing look. My duty at present was not to return it. Hawks are sensitive to the eye and do not like to be regarded. It is their prerogative to regard. The tact of the austringer in this matter was now delightful to me. It was necessary to stand still or to walk gently in the mellow light of the barn, staring straight in front. The attitude was to be conciliatory, yielding, patient, but certain of a firm objective. One was to stand, looking past the hawk into the shadows, making minute and cautious movements, with every faculty on the stretch. There was a rabbit's head in the glove, split in order to show the brains. With this I was to stroke the talons, the chest, the entering of the wings. If it annoyed him in one way I must desist immediately, even before he was annoyed: if in another, so that he would peck at what annoyed him I must continue. Slowly, endlessly, love-givingly, persistently, it was my business to distinguish the annoyances: to stroke and tease the talons, to recite, to make the kindest remonstrances, to flirtingly whistle.

After an hour or two of this, I began to bethink myself. He had already begun to calm down, and would sit on the glove without much bating. But he had suffered a long and terrible journey, so that perhaps it would be better not to 'watch' him (keep him awake) this first night. Perhaps I would let him recuperate a little, free him in the barn, and only come to him at intervals.

It was when I went to him at five minutes past three in the morning, that he stepped voluntary to the fist. Hitherto he had been found in inaccessible places, perched on the highest rafter or flying away from perch to perch. Now, smoothing up to him with stretched hand and imperceptible feet, I was rewarded with a triumph. Gos, with confident but partly disdainful gesture, stepped to the out-feeling glove. He began, not only to peck the rabbit, but distantly to feed.

At ten to five the glow in the small two-shilling lamp was vanquished. Outside, in greyness and dim twilight, the very first birds not sang but moved on their perches. An angler who had been sleepless went past in the half mist to tempt the carp of the lake. He stopped outside the lattice, looked in upon us, but was urged to take his way. Gos bore him fairly well.

He was eating now, pettishly, on the fist, and Rome was not built in a day. Rome was the city in which Tarquin ravished Lucrece; and Gos was Roman as well as Teutonic. He was a Tarquin of the meat he tore, and now the man who owned him decided that he had learned enough. He had met a strange fisherman through the dawning window: he had learned to bite at rabbits' legs: and when he was hungrier he would be more humble.

I came away through the deep dew to make myself a cup of tea: then rapturously, from six until half past nine in the morning, I went to sleep.

T. H. White   83

The Entertainers

Prehistoric man held birds in awe. Ancient kings like Solomon snared and brought them home alive. Greeks kept finches, nightingales, and starlings. In the Renaissance, canaries became popular in Europe and today are the world's leading cage bird. Parrots are next, but most breed only in the wild, where their numbers dwindle as trappers cash in on their popularity.

Trained birds like homing pigeons, falcons, and "talking" birds have contributed much color to our heritage. Cockfighting, perhaps the oldest spectator sport, still draws crowds, even where outlawed. Italians introduced pigeon wars, *la guerra,* to America. Fanciers train their pigeons to intercept other flocks in the air and bring down enemy birds to their rooftops to be captured and bartered or sold.

Birds in captivity may not have benefited much from their unequal partnership with man, but they have provided immeasurable pleasure. Today, zoos give us the joys of observing birds up close and educate us as well about the problems of preserving rare species.

Some animal sports and hobbies that originated in ancient times are still popular today. Cockfighting (left), the origins of which predate Christianity, spread from Asia throughout the world. La guerra (right), a popular sport in Italy in the 16th century, is alive on rooftops in Brooklyn. Centuries after the Greeks began keeping wild songbirds as cage pets, exotic species such as parrots and canaries (above) became popular. Ostriches pull sulkies in Virginia City, Nevada (far left), but in early Egypt, eight of them drew the chariot of King Ptolemy II.

*"In Roman times exotic pets were so common that
. . . an edict had to be promulgated banning tame bears,
boars, panthers and leopards . . . without leashes.
Catullus wrote a famous ode to Lesbia's pet sparrow
and Ovid immortalized his mistress's parrot . . . ."*
RICHARD K. MATHEWS

Never Underestimate the Power of a Pigeon

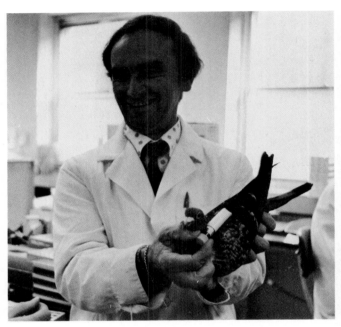

Probably as long as the rock dove, or common pigeon has co-existed with man it has had to struggle against human ignorance. Two of its cousins, the passenger pigeon and the flightless dodo, have already passed into oblivion.

But *Columba livia* is far from extinction; in fact it seems destined to prevail over all other birds. And simply because, centuries ago, it formed an uneasy alliance with man.

Men domesticated the rock dove early in European history. They valued its meat, eggs, feathers and droppings, and found to their delight that the birds offered few maintenance problems.

The Romans were extremely sophisticated in their breeding and raising of the birds, and wealthy patricians owned as many as 10,000. The dovecotes were regularly cleaned and white-washed and, in some cases, contained plumbing to provide running water for the birds.

In later centuries, live pigeons were still an important, pre-refrigeration source of easily raised, maintained and transported protein. Fifteenth-century Fellows of King's College, Cambridge, consumed between two and three thousand pigeon eggs a year.

As Europe moved out of the subsistence standards of the Middle Ages and the Renaissance, its people developed sports and hobbies involving the birds. Nineteenth-century gentlemen shot them in gunning competitions, and developed exotic varieties for show with such names as "pouters," "fantails" and "tumblers." But the most remarkable new pastime was pigeon racing.

Pigeons have been used as messengers for centuries, and Hannibal is alleged to have had carrier birds in his elephant army that crossed the Alps. But it wasn't until the early nineteenth century that this occasional use became a science.

During the first and second world wars, pigeons carried messages in all theaters of action. Birds received such decorations as the Distinguished Service Cross and the Croix de Guerre for their gallantry, and one bird, Cher Ami, saved America's "Lost Battalion." Badly wounded, the pigeon flew 25 miles in 25 minutes.

During World War II, Allied forces dropped their better-trained pigeons with agents, to be used as a more secure and nearly as reliable means of communication as the clandestine radio. The first such pigeon returned from its mission in 1940. She descended with an agent at night, traveled nine miles under the agent's sweater, remained eleven days in concealment, and was finally released the twelfth morning. She was back in her loft by 1500 hours that afternoon with vital information regarding the disposition of enemy troops. For this service, she was decorated with the Dickin Medal, the pigeon's equivalent of the Victoria Cross!

There's little external difference between a racer or carrier pigeon and its feral or wild cousin, the rock dove. The real difference is in some internal mechanism

> *"Pigeons have been used as messengers for centuries, and Hannibal is alleged to have had carrier birds in his elephant army that crossed the Alps. But it wasn't until the early nineteenth century that this occasional use became a science."*

that enables certain birds to return again and again over great distances to a single small space—their loft and nest box. Long races in Europe cover hundreds of miles of air space. And in North America, some contests span 1,500 miles, which the best birds can cover in just three days!

While pigeons normally fly along at a respectable 25 to 35 miles per hour, one English competitor, in 1964, averaged 68.9 mph over a long-distance course. But even this speed was topped by a homer in the United States that turned in a performance of 92 mph. The only birds in the world that can fly faster are falcons.

Increasingly, the pigeon is coming under attack. Since we've evolved cheap chickens, foam pillows and chemical fertilizers, our economy no longer needs pigeons. Thus their abuses and hazards now loom larger in the public's eye than their benefits. Particularly, pigeons are charged with being unhealthy "litter birds."

At least as early as the thirteenth century the bird's roosting and dropping habits were making it unpopular. The acids in pigeon droppings are capable of seriously etching paint, metal and stone surfaces—especially in cities already aggravated by air pollution. In addition, the sheer weight of these droppings can become hazardous. In the mid-1960s, the British Foreign Office had over 50 *tons* of bird excrement removed from its rooftops for fear the added weight of a heavy rain or snowfall would cause the roof to cave in!

Finally, pigeon droppings harbor a variety of bacteria injurious to human health—the most deadly of which is *Cryptococcus neoformans.* The *New York Times* reported that two or three people a year die in the city from streptococcus meningitis, the disease most directly associated with the deadly pigeon-passed spore.

In addition, the birds are fond of pecking at old mortar to get calcium. Since their beaks are not strong enough to make headway on new mortar, it's chiefly the older buildings and monuments that are damaged. All told, pigeons are not exactly desirable city residents.

Despite controls on their populations, such as birth control pills, disease, detergents, and shotguns, pigeons, like people, are in no danger of becoming extinct. Even though Europeans and Americans have abandoned the ornate architecture which once gave the birds ready-made roosting niches, they are now building thousands of highway overpasses and bridges which provide equally good homes. Thus, no matter what form man's progress has taken, pigeons have been more than equal to the challenge of keeping pace.

—George Reiger

Modern telecommunications spelled the end for the U.S. Signal Corps Pigeon Service (opposite, left), but a British laboratory finds that pigeons are invaluable for ferrying blood samples from hospitals (opposite, right). Pigeon races are a popular pastime in Belgium (above, left), and so is shopping for pigeons at outdoor markets (above, right).

The Useful Goose

There is a new type of Scotch Guard in Scotland, and this group wears no kilts! These are the 70-odd white geese who stand guard at the distillery in Dumbarton, Scotland. Led by a cocky old gander called Mr. Ballantine, the geese guard about 30 million gallons of whiskey valued at over 900 million dollars (inclusive of duty). If an intruder were to come near this group, the bedlam of their alarmed chorusing would rival bagpipes themselves.

Found to be more effective than dogs, men or mechanical devices, this web-footed security force also holds economic appeal for the Scotsmen who own the whiskey: they aren't paid wages; they eat grass, need no shelter and lay eggs. They never go out of commission, cause no labor problems and, most important— don't drink Scotch.

Actually this new experiment in Scotland explored an old truth: In the fourth century B.C. geese, one of our oldest domesticated birds, are said to have alerted a city, saved a civilization and changed the course of history. Always versatile and valuable friends of man, they have given us weapons of war, supplied our pens of peace, kept our soldiers warm, prettied up our ladies, and protected our pioneers. In this modern world, geese are also solving some farm problems more efficiently than machines and chemicals. Perhaps the Aesop fable of the goose that laid the golden eggs is more fact than fiction!

We owe the goose a debt of gratitude that could make it our national bird. The settling of America would have been considerably more of a hardship without geese. Many a Conestoga wagon moving West had a pair of the birds aboard. Almost as useful to the pioneers as guns and stout hearts, they required little shelter, could forage for natural food, and seemed to have a high resistance to disease. They were superb watchdogs, safeguarding settler and livestock with their alert bugling which routed many a creeping Indian, as well as wolves, cougars, coyotes and foxes. Goose down lined comforters, feathers made beds warm and soft in those days before furnaces. The bird's abundant fat was butter and lard; it was used as a comforting ointment for rheumatism and aching bones. One goose egg fed two people. The delicate dark meat not only was nutritious but delicious, a welcome change from wild fare.

These remarkable birds are finding new and valuable uses today. Even now, a million geese are at work in the U.S., weeding fields of cotton, potatoes, corn, sugar cane, strawberries, sugar beets, asparagus and nursery plantings. "Goosemation" appears to be the most efficient and economical method of keeping down cotton-choking Johnson grass. A pair of geese effectively clears an acre, eating only grass and weeds; a dozen do the work of one skilled man with a hoe.

Geese are valuable not only for what they can do, but for what they are. Their finest down is still used to make powder puffs; coarser grades go into sleeping bags, comforters, bedding and upholstered furniture. The fat, which has a low melting point, is used by pharmaceutical firms in preparing certain ointments. And who has not drooled over *pâté de foie gras* or roast goose dinner?

Although all true geese fall in but two genera, *Branta* and *Anser,* with more than 40 kinds recognized, ranging worldwide, most of us are aware of only the elegant gray, black and white wild Canada and six domestic breeds admitted to the American Standard of Perfection by the American Poultry Association: Emden, Toulouse, Chinese, African, Canada and Egyptian. With the exception of the Canada and Egyptian, all were developed from the wild graylag. Most unusual are the Crested Roman with its crown of feathers, the curly-plumed Sebastopol, the African Spur-wing with sharp weapon-spurs on the bend of the wings, and the Australian Cape Barren goose that is related to the extinct giant goose of New Zealand. According to most naturalists, however, the goose has lost fewer of its original qualities in over 4,000 years of domestication than any other bird or animal.

I once had a chance to observe the qualities of the wild and the domesticated breeds side by side. One morning my dog, a gentle retriever, came to the kitchen door with a squawking gosling in his mouth, caught probably at a nearby pond where wild Canadas occasionally nested. I put the little goose in a box lined with newspapers and went to the pond to find its parents. But I never found them, so I was stuck as foster father. The gosling, which I named "Backdoor," grew rapidly; in a couple of months I let him run with my Emdens. Developing into a magnificent Canada gander, Backdoor stayed with us for over a year, feeding and freely fraternizing with the domesticated birds.

Naturally we became attached to Backdoor, and naturally, being wild, he left us. One fall afternoon we heard a yelping overhead that sounded like a pack of beagles on a chase. A skein of Canadas was passing up there in their famous V-formation, the late afternoon sun illuminating them like lines of quicksilver against the dark blue of the sky. Backdoor, feeding with the Emdens, raised his head at the sound of the migrating birds, took a few steps, flapped his wings and went into the air. Two Emden ganders

> *"We owe the goose
> a debt of gratitude that
> could make it
> our national bird."*

beside him tried to do the same thing. They never made it, but Backdoor did. The last I saw of him was a tail-ending speck behind the main flock in the darkening sky.

Backdoor had little differences in intelligence, alertness or independence from our popular domesticated geese, and I'm not sure that I would have considered him anything special except for the unusual circumstances of his arrival. The two best known geese in the U.S. are the blue-eyed Emden that orginally came from Germany and the gray-brown Toulouse brought from France.

Wild geese pair for life, but a domestic gander normally mates during his second year with two females. After a noisy courtship, the females pull that priceless down from their breast to line the ground nests, each laying from 12 to 60 white, 8-ounce eggs between February and late June. Compared with a chicken that lays perhaps 300 eggs a year but is finished at three, the goose is a wonder, still going strong at age ten or more.

One goose breeder told me how clever the birds were about protecting their eggs. The female hovers the nest for 28 days, spelled by the gander while she goes for food and water. They prefer to hover a large clutch — 15 to 20 eggs. He watched a pair build a nest in the barn; then they left this nest, and, working together, dug a deep cave near a pond on the edge of some woods. He looked every day for the eggs in the barn or cave, but they never appeared. It was weeks until he found the real nest, well-hidden, many yards from the other two areas. He told me these were common diversionary tactics geese employ to evade their enemies. He also knew when the eggs were about to hatch. The gander went on guard duty the night before the goslings were born, then stayed close to them until they were well feathered. Goslings begin foraging for food within 24 hours, are on their own in less than two months.

According to one theory, those fabulous goose feathers are waterproofed by a method called "preening," with the goose distributing oil from a rear gland with the bill. Air trapped in feathers, aided by air sacs in the body, helps the goose to swim well. When they first enter water domestic geese usually dive, staying submerged for 10 seconds. I've watched them do this a dozen times before they are content to come up and paddle. One of my geese would go under like a seal and swim across the pond before he surfaced. Then he would repeat the performance, popping up as close to me as he could.

When geese are feeding in water, transverse toothlike ridges on the inside edge of the bill strain food from mud

AMERICAN WHITE-FRONTED GOOSE.

"...*people who have geese seldom consider them*
mere barnyard creatures like a chicken, a duck or a turkey.
A goose is a loyal helper and friend....
Whoever coined that phrase 'silly as a goose'
obviously never spent any time with geese."

and water. The sharp edge of the bill is used for cutting grass—as effectively as a mechanical clipper. If they are supplied with pasture, geese are almost self-supporting after 4 months. Unlike their closest relatives, ducks and swans, they are not gluttons. Where they have access to pasture, farmers can put a week's rations out, knowing that the birds will eat only a day's supply at one time.

Geese are long-lived, sometimes living to be 40 or so. Shrewd and courageous, they will attack almost anything that molests them or their young. One goose remained on her nest guarding her eggs, fighting a pig until she was killed. My two Emden faced down a fox (their deadly enemy), keeping the quick, clever animal at bay with flips of their strong wings and snake-like hissings.

In time of danger, geese often work in pairs, the gander taking the initiative, extending his neck, lowering it to the ground, trumpeting until he drives the intruder away. If he needs help the female rushes in. He returns with a lordly waddle and loud bugling, echoed by the female in what is called the "triumph ceremony."

They are naturally belligerent and can't be bluffed or cowed, but are seemingly aware when you are intimidated. I saw four Toulouse rout a six-foot electrician atop his car, keeping him there until the farmer's five-year-old son came and shooed them away. A wing-blow from any of the birds could have sent the boy tumbling. But he was their friend, so they went meekly.

Geese also seem to have a sense of humor. Six domestic Canadas on a Connecticut estate delighted in trapping guests in the swimming pool, running around the edge hissing and flapping their wings when a swimmer tried to get out. As the trapped person began calling for help and they heard their owner approaching, they would waddle off in dignified single file.

The goose's sense of hearing is remarkable. A writer friend has a German shepherd, a breed with upright ears that have superb parabolic reflecting ability to catch sounds. This dog would hear and recognize my friend's wife's car a half mile away as it changed gears to start up the steep hill leading to their home. But his pair of geese would recognize the sound of her motor before she shifted gears—perhaps a mile away—and start honking. But they ignored other traffic.

Their sight is just as keen. Dr. J. S. Phillips has observed his tame Canadas search the sky, then focus on a spot and call to a wedge of wild geese so high that no human eye would have noticed them.

Many even believe that this alertness saved an empire from toppling. When the Roman armies invaded Britain in the first century B.C., they found the wild graylag goose domesticated. Impressed with its possibilities, they brought some of the birds back to Italy. They proved to be their most valuable plunder.

Three centuries later the Gauls swept through Italy, driving back the vaunted Roman armies until only a single garrison was left to make a stand on the Capitoline Hill in Rome. Late one night, according to the legend, the Gauls noiselessly climbed the steep cliff leading up the Capitoline. At the summit, they fed the starving watchdogs to keep them quiet, then crept toward the sleeping garrison, unaware that a gaggle of graylag geese, sacred to Juno, had the run of the Hill.

Suddenly there were shrill calls and honkings. The Roman soldiers sprang into action. The invaders, who had counted on surprise as their chief weapon, were themselves surprised, and routed from Rome.

Geese do have a special way of putting you in their debt. One gander appointed himself Sunday guardian of an aged blind woman, walking her to church, taking the hem of her dress to direct her. During church services he cropped grass in the nearby cemetery. When she was ready he guided his mistress home.

A curious fact about geese, discovered by the Viennese naturalist, Konrad Z. Lorenz, who has made a study of them for many years, is that they will adopt as their parent the first thing they see when they leave the egg. By imitating the sounds and actions of the female, Lorenz has mothered many gaggles of newborn goslings. It is an amusing sight to see the dignified, bearded scientist walking and even swimming with the goslings following him everywhere.

This friendly trait is so strong that people who have geese seldom consider them mere barnyard creatures like a chicken, a duck or a turkey. A goose is a loyal helper and friend. For geese have done more than guard, amuse, feed and clothe us; they have enriched our language with fable, folklore, idiom and proverb. Whoever coined that phrase "silly as a goose" obviously never spent any time with geese.

———————————— Jack Denton Scott

Farmers and manufacturers are discovering that man's best friend may be a goose. A hissing, cackling, wing-beating goose (top left) makes an excellent watchdog. That is why a Scotch-whiskey distiller employs a platoon of them to guard its warehouses near Glasgow (middle and bottom left). In California, geese are used to crop weeds in cotton fields (middle right). Adult birds spend the night at a cotton-hauling trailer that doubles as shelter and a watering spot (bottom right), but the goslings (top right) are returned to warm brooder houses at night.

Flights
of
Inspiration

The Artist's View

Artists and naturalists alike have for millenia been inspired by birds—by their colors, their freedom of the air. In early America, sharp-eyed observers tried to document the diversity of bird life in the New World. They also wanted to bring to their paintings a vitality that would lift them out of the category of mere illustration. Today we enjoy many of these works as much for their beauty as for their scientific accuracy. The prints shown here are but a sampling of the great bird portraits that continue to enrich us all.

reus Efculi divifura, Foliis
lioribus aculeatis. *Pluk: Hift.*   *Red Oak.*

Palumbus Migratorius.
The Pigeon of Paßage.

". . . who can either respect, pity or admire what they are totally unacquainted with?"
ALEXANDER WILSON

Mark Catesby (1682-1749?) painted the passenger pigeon (left, below) as part of an attempt to catalog birds of southeastern North America, but historians have pointed out that his most notable achievement was artistic, not scientific. He used birds "as part of a larger decorative pattern of flowers and plants." Later, Alexander Wilson (1766-1813) also broke new ground with his grouse portrait (left, above) by modeling his work on a live subject observed in the wild. Within a few years Catesby's technique and Wilson's fieldwork would be combined by John James Audubon (1785-1851), who sought to recreate "nature, alive and moving." His osprey with trout at right is a vivid masterpiece.

"CHINESE GOLDEN PHEASANT" BY FRANCIS LEE JAQUES (1887-1969), N.D.; LEFT, "GYRFALCON," 1910 (TOP), AND "EASTERN KINGBIRD," PRE-1915 (BOTTOM), BY LOUIS AGASSIZ FUERTES. OPPOSITE: "GREEN HERONS AND LUNA MOTH" BY JOHN JAMES AUDUBON, 1821 OR 1822.

Audubon's **Birds of America,** which included the green heron opposite, set an extremely high standard for wildlife illustration. By the end of the nineteenth century, however, an heir to his legacy had been found: Louis Agassiz Fuertes (1874-1927). Even before he had graduated from Cornell in 1897, Fuertes had three books to his credit; and such accomplished works as the gyrfalcon and Eastern kingbird (left, top and bottom) would follow. Francis Lee Jaques (1887-1969), who produced the Chinese golden pheasant above, began painting birds in earnest only at 37, after a career that ranged from working in a shipyard to being a taxidermist.

© Roger Tory Peterson — '76

Nature "... should be interpreted by those
who know something about their subject
and feel deeply about it. A painting is
a composite of the artist's past experience."

ROGER TORY PETERSON

Many bird artists knew birds intimately long before they began to paint them. Roger Tory Peterson's high school yearbook said of the boy who was to paint snowy owls (opposite): "Here are the makings of a great naturalist." Don Eckelberry hunted, but found drawing spruce grouse (above left) more to his liking. As a hunter and outdoorsman, Maynard Reece developed an eye for pheasants (left). George Miksch Sutton brought the knowledge of zoology to his portrait of the warbler named after him (above right).

"The heroes of my early painting days were Brooks, Fuertes and Thorburn; much later came my admiration for John James Audubon. I took something from each of them and developed or adapted it in my own way, to fit my own needs."

J. FENWICK LANSDOWNE

An artist, said Degas, "does not draw what he sees, but what he must make others see." The physical characteristics of a bird are obvious, but it is difficult to show, as Basil Ede has done in his duck painting (left), the effort expended by the bird as it struggles against gravity to leave the clinging surface of a pond. J. Fenwick Lansdowne catches the tension in a flighty warbler as it pauses momentarily on a flower stem (bottom far left), and Chuck Ripper shows us the lethal intensity of a great horned owl (top far left), staring balefully from its high perch.

"MALLARD" BY BASIL EDE, 1964. OPPOSITE: TOP, "GREAT HORNED OWL" BY CHUCK RIPPER, 1973; BOTTOM, "GOLDEN-WINGED WARBLER" BY J. FENWICK LANSDOWNE, 1969.

The American Eagle

From its very first appearance as our national emblem, the eagle as a decorative motif has held precedence over all other designs, and today its popularity has not diminished. The folk art of New England took on a fresh outlook with the adoption of the American eagle as the national symbol of the United States. Every craftsman in the then sprawling Republic was eager to depict the *royal* bird in one form or another. The potter, the signmaker, the woodcarver, the glassmaker, the printer, the weaver, the buttonmaker, and all the other skilled artisans of the day wasted no time in imprinting their new symbol of freedom on everything that they made. The housewife, not to be outdone, proudly displayed the great bird on her quilts, her rugs, her embroidery, and other kinds of needlework.

The new symbol was distinctive in form—signifying virility, strength, pride, majesty. It represented, in a sense, the kind of uplift which the battle-weary colonists needed after their struggle. At the close of the Revolution, the adoption of the American eagle, the symbol of Liberty, was truly a god-send to the colonists of New England and the rest of rough-hewn America. As the eagle soared, so, too, did the spirits of these freedom-loving people. In 1789 when George Washington made his triumphant tour of the colonies, transparent painted eagles sketched on paper were placed against the window panes of houses everywhere along his route, with lighted candles behind them. Even their oppressors in the fatherland, quick to sense the pulse of the new nation and eager to recapture the promising market, soon flooded the colonies with goods of every description—clocks, fabrics, buttons, china, glass—marked with the new symbol of hope and freedom.

Later, when New England sea captains opened the China trade, the imperious bird in highly stylized form appeared on all types of fine china, often in gold. In many ways, the extensive and unrestrained use of the national emblem in every conceivable manner during the early days of the Republic set a precedent for the advertising techniques of later generations.

As a decorative feature, on sofas, bedposts, the backs of chairs, match boxes, in stencil designs, rugs, wallpaper, on door knockers, tavern signs, pitchers, bowls, and dozens of other household articles, the eagle appeared in some form. The ancient warrior bird soared sunward in their hearts and was everywhere present as a symbol of courage and endurance to express the independence which they cherished so dearly.

The eagle was a familiar insignia on tavern signs throughout the country, so that no traveler foreign or native was unmindful of the new-found freedom symbol. Edward Everett Hale, noted Boston preacher and writer, recalled his summer visit to northern Vermont in the 1850's. In describing the signs, he wrote: "Almost without exception their devices were of the American eagle with his wings spread, or of the American eagle holding the English lion in chains, or of the lion chained without any American eagle."

Early in the 19th century Putman and Roff, a firm manufacturing paper hangings and band boxes in Connecticut, designed a trade-mark featuring the eagle. Since no special etiquette had been devised for the national emblem, the eagle was utilized to carry the firm name on a ribbon in the bird's mouth and claws. (This was common practice with many craftsmen and tradesmen who made use of the eagle to advertise their wares.)

Free-standing eagles carved from wood or made of metal in various sizes and usually gilded have had strong eye appeal since the late eighteenth century. Their decorative uses are legion and the notable examples that have survived are greatly cherished. Samuel McIntire (1757-1811), noted architect and woodcarver of Salem, Massachusetts, made a number of them for public buildings and the cupolas of carriage houses. McIntire trained and inspired other craftsmen to carve eagles, among them Joseph True of Salem. True carved the imposing specimen that adorns the Salem Custom House where Nathaniel Hawthorne wrote the preface to *The Scarlet Letter* while serving as Collector.

New England's most distinguished carver of eagles was John Haley Bellamy (1836-1914), often referred to as "The Woodcarver of Kittery Point, Maine." He worked in the heyday of the eagle in naval design and produced many notable birds including the figurehead for the U.S.S. *Lancaster* with a wingspread of eighteen feet. His work was characterized by the kind of individuality that has given rise to the term "Bellamy Eagle." Even when he carved eagles for public buildings, they were usually draped with the flag. His talent was characterized by great facility and speed and he turned out flocks of small eagles measuring two feet across which he gave to friends and neighbors. Until recent years, practically every house in Kittery Point had an eagle on display.

Now, after more than a century and a half, there are those who would scrap the American eagle as our national emblem and substitute for it the Statue of Liberty. In the *New York Times,* February 14, 1960, Professor Richard B. Morris of Columbia University wrote a lengthy plea for abolishing the eagle as our national symbol on the basis of its being un-American. Resorting to Benjamin Franklin's claim, he declared that the big bird was "lazy, cowardly, rapacious, and hardly a fit national emblem." As a suitable symbol, he advocated the image of Liberty —based on Bartholdi's famous statue at the entrance to New York Harbor. His impassioned plea did not go unanswered. Most readers who replied to the plea took a firm stand in favor of the eagle as an outstanding bird and a worthy and appropriate symbol.

Priscilla Sawyer Lord
and Daniel J. Foley

The simple painting on a tavern sign (opposite) and the patriotic carving on President Lincoln's barge (top) are only two of thousands of decorative uses to which the bald eagle has been put since its adoption for the Great Seal of the United States. A modern woodcarver (right) continues the tradition as he chisels an eagle motif for a ship.

America's Native Wildlife Art Form

Somewhere back in time, an aboriginal hunter watched the way that flying ducks often landed near flocks of feeding ducks, and he had an idea. Why not make some imitation ducks and float them on a likely-looking piece of water? So he did, and it worked, and the first decoys were created.

That probably happened several thousand years ago. Unfortunately, the hero of the story is a victim of historical obscurity. Matter of fact, history doesn't even record his nationality.

But one thing's for sure: decoys can stake out a just claim to be truly American. Only in America were decoys developed and used on a broad scale, so it's not stretching a point to call them an indigenous American folk art. Even the word "decoy" is American, probably derived from a Dutch expression, *Ende-Kooy,* meaning duck cage or trap.

The idea of luring birds with decoys was already in use by the Indians when the white man arrived. Decoys fashioned of tule reeds and stuffed skins found in caves in Nevada dated back more than 1,000 years.

About 1800, a few wooden decoys started to appear on the American hunting scene. They were crude efforts and the most one could say for them is that they were more durable than the Indians' reed jobs.

Although individual rigs of wood decoys were in use from 1800 to 1850, the golden age of decoy ducks and shorebirds began in the last half of the century. There were two reasons for this increased use of decoys: The development of breech loading firearms, which made wing shooting practical and economical; and the appearance of the market hunter.

How and why did market gunning start? Hunger and economics. With the advent of the Industrial Revolution, Americans concentrated more in large cities and towns. Although they didn't have the opportunity to shoot waterfowl, they still had a taste for them and were willing to pay to sate their appetites. Millions of waterfowl were slaughtered for fancy restaurants and meat markets. Wild ducks and geese were common fare on most menus, and plover, curlew and yellowlegs were almost as easily available.

To the meat hunters, tools of the trade were mighty important. No matter whether they shot from a boat or a blind, decoys and bait brought in the birds. Is it any wonder that great care was lavished on a hunter's decoys?

Market hunters and sportsmen developed specific terms for decoys and decoying. Shorebird decoys were often called "stools" and duck decoys were sometimes referred to as "blocks" or "tollers." A rig consisted of a group of decoys, of one or more species, designed to be set out to attract birds. Rigs varied from huge spreads of 400 decoys or more to tidy shorebird rigs of six or eight stick-ups. "Stick-ups" are so called because, as the name implies, the decoys were placed on sticks. Eight or ten artfully placed stick-ups were irresistible to plover, curlew, snipe, yellowlegs and other birds.

Names like the Great South Bay, Barnegat, Stratford, Chesapeake, Cobb's Island, Cape Cod, Delaware and Illinois Rivers are not geography to the decoy collector. Rather they represent specific styles of decoys each with peculiar regional characteristics.

There are a number of reasons for these regional differences. Practical usage under different water conditions dictated certain structural designs. Decoys from the Stratford, Connecticut, area have an exaggerated overhanging breast designed to ride the slush ice that comes down the river. Stratford decoys are of hollow construction and invariably carry a teardrop-shaped lead weight on the bottom for ballast. Their heads are low, as are many decoys of the Delaware River.

Probably the main reason for regional characteristics —even more than water conditions—was the fact that the best local carver usually taught others and loaned out his patterns. For example, Albert Laing of Stratford, Connecticut (1811-1885) was a carpenter by trade but an avid shooter and an unusually skillful decoy carver. He started the style known as "Stratford" which was carried on by such apt students as Holmes and, of course, Charles "Shang" Wheeler. Wheeler was a master carver whose work was the forerunner of the decorative mantelpiece "decoys" of today.

There were many market gunners whose decoy carving far surpassed the fame of their shooting. The most famous of these from Barnegat Bay in New Jersey was Harry Shourdes. Shourdes turned out many thousands of decoys and shipped them to every state in the Union. His skill at selecting cedar is evident in the beautiful condition of the Shourdes decoys that repose on collectors' shelves today—nary a crack or a check.

Barnegat brant and black duck decoys have a special flair and sleekness that gives them a charm and look all their own. A Barnegat decoy is quickly identifiable by the well-rounded tail, the upright head, the lightness (they are hollow and thin walled), the countersunk lead weight in the bottom, and the smoothness and finish.

Other areas that are famous for decoys include Cape Cod, home of the king of New England's makers, Elmer

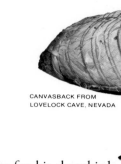

CANVASBACK FROM
LOVELOCK CAVE, NEVADA

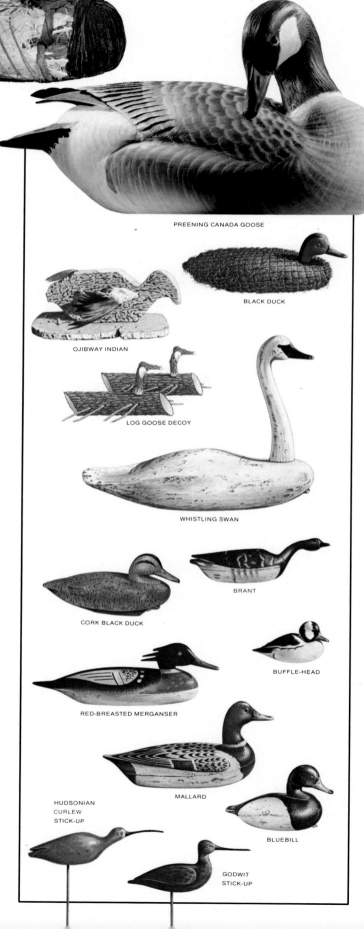

PREENING CANADA GOOSE

BLACK DUCK

OJIBWAY INDIAN

LOG GOOSE DECOY

WHISTLING SWAN

BRANT

CORK BLACK DUCK

BUFFLE-HEAD

RED-BREASTED MERGANSER

MALLARD

HUDSONIAN
CURLEW
STICK-UP

BLUEBILL

GODWIT
STICK-UP

Crowell. Elmer is even more famous for his shorebirds than his ducks and a Crowell decoy commands a premium price today far beyond any price their maker would have dreamed possible for his work.

The list of makers and famous decoy areas wouldn't be complete without mentioning Chesapeake canvasbacks, the whittling Cobb family of Cobb's Island, Virginia, and from nearby Chincoteague Island, the names of Ira Hudson and Doug Jester. Possibly the greatest carvers of that area are the Ward Brothers of Crisfield, Maryland, who still whittle today [1967], although they are at an age when most folks have long been retired.

Just how much of a likeness decoys must bear to their live counterparts is a much-argued question. Some hunters maintain that the more realistic the decoy, the better the hunting. Others argue most vehemently that a decoy that captures the "feeling" of the live bird works equally well. Some snow goose hunters do well with decoys made simply of balled-up newspapers. It's from such delightful differences of opinion that the fun of folk art is created.

The romance of names and places, anecdotes, stories and tales of the days of America's great waterfowling are as much a lure to the decoy collector as the art of the decoy itself. Decoys tell the history of American waterfowl hunting, but even if you are not a hunter or historian, decoys can be enjoyed as a folk art in their own right.

That decoys merit serious consideration as art can be testified to by the fact that more and more natural history, folk art and general art museums are including permanent decoy exhibits.

And while hundreds of thousands of decoys were made, only a few can be classified as outstanding pieces of art. I've spent days looking through as many as a thousand decoys without finding a collectible item that had history or art enough to recommend it to posterity.

There are still decoys waiting to be discovered, however. In decoy country, every old attic, barn, basement, shed and waterfront shanty holds the prospect of a possible find. Lying mute and captive in a gunny sack somewhere are some great decoys just waiting to be liberated. Maybe one or more of them will wind up on a mantel or shelf in your home. Good hunting!

—Ralph Loeff

Decoys, a uniquely American art form, have been made with everything from reeds lashed together by Indian hunters (top) to wood intricately carved and painted by professional artists (second from top).

The Dodo.

Geo Edwards, Sculp: A.D. 175

294

Birds and Words

Some of us, whether hawks or doves, forceful or peaceful, get up with the birds, swallow a quick breakfast—"not enough to keep a sparrow healthy"—and fly to the station, wondering why the old coot ahead of us doesn't drive more carefully.

We take a flyer to town, and note that the boss is watching us like a hawk as we mince pigeon-toed between the desks.

At lunch, we chicken out on a fellow worker's challenge to take the afternoon off for a round of golf, although we know we could certainly score a birdie or two and perhaps an eagle.

After a brace of cocktails when we return to the family nest, we feel light as a feather and free as a bird and cock of the walk. We may seem talky as a parrot to our wives, but on the morrow we'll be eating crow. And so to bed—also with the birds.

Sometimes we get the bird. We know what that means, but we may not know that originally this was a British expression, "to get the big bird," the big bird being the goose and the reference being to the hissing sound made by geese when excited.

Those of us who are entertainers know we get the bird when we lay an egg and for us, that week, no eagle will fly—there will be no payday.

We use other expressions. The cockpit of an airplane got its name from the pit into which cocks were dropped when two were pitted against each other. The term, to "show the white feather," comes from cockfighting, where crossbred fighting cocks often had white feathers and usually were defeated by purebred cocks having coats of solid black or red feathers. At the moment of defeat, the crest of the beaten cock would droop limply—and thus originated the word "crestfallen."

A somewhat more amiable sport gave rise to the word "lark." In the time of Shakespeare, many people regarded the lark as one of the most toothsome items of game. Since larks are too small for hunting—at least with the weapons then available—they were usually trapped in nets. The nets were set out before daybreak, and the larks were enmeshed when they came down to feed.

It was not uncommon for young men and young women to join in the enterprise, and because their early morning activities sometimes were not wholly limited to trapping the birds, the whole business soon took on the aspects of an outdoor frolic, and larking became as popular as discotheques are today.

Some birds, in Shelley's phrase, "never wert." Among them are Lewis Carroll's "slithy toves" and Cape Cod

turkey—codfish, which got its fanciful name the same way, and for the same reasons, that a dish of melted cheese on toast came to be called Welsh rabbit. And then there is Scotch woodcock, which simply consists of scrambled eggs heaped on toast spread with anchovy butter.

We have some special names for groups of birds. Just as we call a group of lions a pride of lions, we speak of a gaggle of geese and a covey of partridges or quail. Most of these labels are obsolete now, but in days when hunting was a quest for food rather than recreation, such distinctions in the labeling of bird groups were observed carefully. The true birdwatcher would speak of a nye of pheasants, a cast of hawks, and a watch of nightingales. Peacocks, appropriately enough, assemble in a muster, coots in covert, and larks in an exaltation.

The gull through the ages has been synonymous with a person easily tricked, cheated, or duped. Similarly pigeon—a bird not dissimilar in appearance to the gull—long has been underworld slang for a person waiting to be fleeced or plucked. The stool pigeon, though, is a bird of slightly different feathers. The stool in this case is a pole to which a bird is fastened in order to decoy other birds. The original stool pigeon in underworld slang, then, was a spy the law planted among outlaws.

The "cock" in "cocker spaniel" comes from woodcock, a small bird for the hunting of which this breed of spaniel was widely used.

Dozens of similes and analogies are related to birds: Chattering like magpies, hoarse as a crow, sweet as a nightingale, feather in your cap, crow's nest (of a ship), to crow about, as the crow flies, swansong, bird-brain, eagle-eyed, egghead, as welcome as a robin in spring, one swallow doesn't make a summer, robin's-egg blue, eggshell white, duck soup, to crane, to duck, goose flesh, swan-necked, graceful as a swan, hawk-eyed, sparrowlike, soft as down, dove-tail, night-owl, gooseneck, cock-and-bull, cook one's goose, ducks and drakes, lame duck, popinjay, one fell swoop, talk turkey, roost, chicken-hearted.

You know many other terms of, by, and for the birds: Bluebird weather, wild-goose chase, black as a crow, weather fit for ducks, stormy petrel, free as a bird, feather your nest, a high flyer, the turkey trot, dead as a dodo, like water on a duck's back, light as a feather, cock of the walk, bird of passage, bird of peace, and bird's-eye view.

Maybe some of them will enlarge your view.

William Morris

"THE DODO" BY GEORGE EDWARDS, 1757.

Through the Eyes of Poets

Seagulls

Between the under and the upper blue
All day the seagulls climb and swerve and soar,
Arc intersecting arc, curve over curve.

And you may watch them weaving a long time
And never see their pattern twice the same
And never see their pattern once imperfect.

Take any moment they are in the air—
If you could change them, if you had the power
How would you place them other than they are?

What we have labored all our lives to have
And failed, these birds effortlessly achieve;
Freedom that flows in form and still is free.

ROBERT FRANCIS

Pigeons

They paddle with staccato feet
In powder-pools of sunlight,
Small blue busybodies
Strutting like fat gentlemen
With hands clasped
Under their swallowtail coats;
And, as they stump about,
Their heads like tiny hammers
Tap at imaginary nails
In non-existent walls.
Elusive ghosts of sunshine
Slither down the green gloss
Of their necks an instant, and are gone.

Summer hangs drugged from sky to earth
In limpid fathoms of silence:
Only warm dark dimples of sound
Slide like slow bubbles
From the contented throats.

Raise a casual hand—
With one quick gust
They fountain into air.

RICHARD KELL

Twilight Whippoorwill . . .
Whistle on, sweet deepener
Of dark loneliness.

BASHO

SOOTY TERNS

A Bird Came Down the Walk

A bird came down the walk:
He did not know I saw;
He bit an angle-worm in halves
And ate the fellow, raw.

And then he drank a dew
From a convenient grass,
And then hopped sidewise
  to the wall
To let a beetle pass.

He glanced with rapid eyes
That hurried all abroad,—
They looked like frightened beads,
  I thought
He stirred his velvet head

Like one in danger; cautious,
I offered him a crumb,
And he unrolled his feathers
And rowed him softer home

Than oars divide the ocean,
Too silver for a seam,
Or butterflies, off banks of noon,
Leap, plashless, as they swim.

EMILY DICKINSON

Something Told the Wild Geese

Something told the wild geese
  It was time to go.
Though the fields lay golden
  Something whispered,—"Snow."
Leaves were green and stirring,
  Berries, luster-glossed,
But beneath warm feathers
  Something cautioned,—"Frost."
All the sagging orchards
  Steamed with amber spice,
But each wild breast stiffened
  At remembered ice.
Something told the wild geese
  It was time to fly,—
Summer sun was on their wings,
  Winter in their cry.

RACHEL FIELD

The Darkling Thrush

I leant upon a coppice gate
  When Frost was specter-gray,
And Winter's dregs made desolate
  The weakening eye of day.
The tangled bine-stems scored the sky
  Like strings of broken lyres,
And all mankind that haunted nigh
  Had sought their household fires.

The land's sharp features seemed to be
  The Century's corpse outleant,
His crypt the cloudy canopy,
  The wind his death-lament.
The ancient pulse of germ and birth
  Was shrunken hard and dry;
And every spirit upon earth
  Seemed fervorless as I.

At once a voice arose among
  The bleak twigs overhead
In a full-hearted evensong
  Of joy illimited;
An aged thrush, frail, gaunt, and small,
  In blast-beruffled plume,
Had chosen thus to fling his soul
  Upon the growing gloom.

So little cause for carolings
  Of such ecstatic sound
Was written on terrestrial things
  Afar or nigh around,
That I could think there trembled through
  His happy good-night air
Some blessed Hope, whereof he knew
  And I was unaware.

THOMAS HARDY

The Eagle (Fragment)

He clasps the crag with crooked hands;
Close to the sun in lonely lands,
Ring'd with the azure world, he stands.

The wrinkled sea beneath him crawls;
He watches from his mountain walls;
And like a thunderbolt he falls.

ALFRED, LORD TENNYSON

The Birds of America

Said the Birds of America:
    quak quek quark quark, hoo hoo
rarrp rarrp, gogogogock
feebee, cheep cheep, kakakaa
coo ahh, choo eee, coo coo!

And what is the meaning of that?
said the solemn Birdcage Maker.

O nothing at all, said the Old Turkey,
we just enjoy the noise.

Why not do something that makes some sense?
said the serious Birdcage Man.

    We do, we do, all there is to do,
said the Eagle, the Lark, and the others:
    We eat and sleep and move about
    and watch what's going on.
    We mate and nest and sit and hatch
    and watch the young get on.
    We hunt and preen and sing and wash,
    we take long journeys and local jaunts
    or simply sit about and scratch
    and watch what's going on.

That's quite pointless! said the Birdcage Man,
You'll never get anywhere that way.

Maybe, said the Magpie.
    But when this continent began
we birds were the only two-legged creatures
and we're still very much around.

What's more, the Woodpecker added,
everything man knows he learned from us birds
but he's never enjoyed it as much.

The Cagemaker scoffed:
    What could I learn from you?

    To do, to do, all there is to do,
said the Heron, the Crow and the others:
    To eat and sleep and move about
    and watch what's going on.
    To mate and nest and sit and hatch
    and watch the young get on.
    To hunt and preen and sing and wash,
    to take long journeys and local jaunts
    or simply sit about and scratch
    and watch what's going on.

O that's absurd! said the Birdcage Maker,
Don't you know the real meaning of life?

Of course we do, said the Birds of America:
    quak quek quark quark, hoo hoo
rarrp rarrp, gogogogock
feebee, cheep cheep, kakakaaa
coo ahh, choo eee, coo coo!

JAMES BROUGHTON

Ducks' Ditty

All along the backwater,
Through the rushes tall,
Ducks are a-dabbling,
Up tails all!

Ducks' tails, drakes' tails,
Yellow feet a-quiver,
Yellow bills all out of sight
Busy in the river!

Slushy green undergrowth
Where the roach swim—
Here we keep our larder,
Cool and full and dim.

Every one for what he likes!
We like to be
Heads down, tails up,
Dabbling free!

High in the blue above
Swifts whirl and call—
We are down a-dabbling
Up tails all!

KENNETH GRAHAME

The Ptarmigan

The ptarmigan is strange,
As strange as he can be;
Never sits on ptelephone poles
Or roosts upon a ptree.
And the way he ptakes
    pto spelling
Is the strangest thing pto me.

ANONYMOUS

Fable of the Talented Mockingbird

Said the little warbling vireo
To the talented mockingbird
Your Vireo Variations are
Among the best I've heard!

You mockingbirds are amazing!
Said the southern chickadee
Your version of my legato
Is remarkably like me!

You ought to become a professional!
Remarked the Florida jay
Allow me to be your promoter
At twenty acorns a day!

The mockingbird sat in a cypress
When the moon was over the wood
And sang an original love song
That nobody understood.

SCOTT BATES

The Wild Swans at Coole

The trees are in their autumn beauty,
The woodland paths are dry,
Under the October twilight the water
Mirrors a still sky;
Upon the brimming water among the stones
Are nine-and-fifty swans.

The nineteenth autumn has come upon me
Since first I made my count;
I saw, before I had well finished
All suddenly mount
And scatter wheeling in great broken rings
Upon their clamorous wings.

I have looked upon those brilliant creatures,
And now my heart is sore.
All's changed since I, hearing at twilight,
The first time on this shore,
The bell-beat of their wings above my head,
Trod with a lighter tread.

Unwearied still, lover by lover,
They paddle in the cold
Companionable streams or climb the air;
Passion or conquest, wander where they will,
Attend upon them still.

But now they drift on the still water,
Mysterious, beautiful;
Among what rushes will they build,
By what lake's edge or pool
Delight men's eyes when I awake some day
To find they have flown away?

WILLIAM BUTLER YEATS

The Bird of Night

A shadow is floating through the moonlight.
Its wings don't make a sound.
Its claws are long, its beak is bright.
Its eyes try all the corners of the night.

It calls and calls: all the air swells and heaves
And washes up and down like water.
The ear that listens to the owl believes
In death. The bat beneath the eaves,

The mouse beside the stone are still as death.
The owl's air washes them like water.
The owl goes back and forth inside the night,
And the night holds its breath.

RANDALL JARRELL

November sunrise . . .
Uncertain, the cold storks stand . . .
Bare sticks in water.

KAKEI

110

BLUEBIRDS HUDDLED IN HOLLOWED-OUT LOG

The Gods Had Wings

That fertility of imagination which has given us the unicorn and the centaur has not failed to fill the air with birds which never owed their origin to any egg. Conceived in error, incubated in ignorance, and hatched into the credulous nest of the primitive mind, they have not wholly ceased from flying in the further corners of the earth.

The Roc

Some fabulous birds are due, no doubt, to travellers' tales. In the far off days, he who had been hardy enough to venture from his own land must needs justify his journey when he returned, and there was no point in spoiling the description of a new bird for the lack of a few picturesque details. Sinbad's story of the gigantic roc's egg, and the bird to whose leg he bound himself with his sash is perhaps an example, and is too well known to need retelling. But he was not the inventor of this. There lay a rooted idea in the minds of the people of that part that such a bird did exist, and Marco Polo heard of it on his

travels. He says

'The people of the island (Madagascar) report that at a certain season of the year an extraordinary kind of bird, which they call a *rukh,* makes its appearance from the southern region. In form it is said to resemble the eagle, but it is incomparably greater in size; being so large and strong as to seize an elephant with its talons, and to lift it into the air, from whence it lets it fall to the ground, in order that when dead it may prey upon the carcase. Persons who have seen this bird assert that when the wings are spread they measure sixteen paces in extent from point to point, and that the feathers are eight paces in length and thick in proportion. The Grand Khan, having heard this extraordinary relation, sent messengers to the island . . . to examine into the circumstances of the country and the truth of the wonderful things told of it. When they returned to the presence of His Majesty they brought with them (as I have heard) a feather of the *rukh,* positively affirmed to have measured ninety spans.'

The Phoenix

In the days when poets sought their similes more from their books than from nature around them, the phoenix had to work overtime. Phebe says in *As You Like It,* that she would not marry Roselind 'Were men as rare as Phoenix'; and John Lyly, with whom unnatural natural history was a hobby, has the following lines in his *Euphues:*

> There is a bird that builds its nest with spice
>   And built, the sun to ashes doth her burn,
> Out of whose cinders doth another rise,
>   And she by scorching beams to dust doth turn.

Pliny gives a full, though rather sceptical, account of the bird. He calls it '. . . That famous bird of Arabia, though I am not quite sure its existence is not all a fable. It is said that there is only one in existence in the whole world, and that that one has not been seen very often. We are told that this bird is the size of an eagle, and has a brilliant golden plumage about the neck, while the rest of the body is of a purple colour, except the tail, which is azure with long feathers intermixed of a roseate hue; the throat is adorned with a crest, and the head with a tuft of feathers. No person has ever seen this bird eat. In Arabia it is looked upon as sacred to the sun, and it lives five hundred and forty years. When it becomes old, it builds a nest of cassia and sprigs of incense, which it fills with perfumes, and then lays its body down to die. From its bones and marrow there springs at first a sort

of small worm which in time changes into a little bird. The first thing it does is to perform the obsequies of its predecessor, and to carry the nest entire to Heliopolis, and there deposit it upon the altar of that divinity (the Sun).' Manlius, from whom he quotes, says: 'The revolution of the great year is completed with the life of this bird, and then a new cycle comes round with the same characteristics as the former one in the seasons and the appearance of the stars. (Computed variously from 500 to 560 years.) This bird was brought to Rome in the censorship of the Emperor Claudius, A.U.C. 800, and was exposed to public view in the Comitium. This fact is attested by the Public Annals, but there is no one that doubts that it was a fictitious phoenix only.'

The phoenix was usually understood to sit on the date palm, and there to die and revive again. In Egypt the palm was the symbol of triumph, but among the early Christians it meant martyrdom. The early fathers referred to Christ as the phoenix. In the Bestiary of Philippe de Thaum we find the following remarks about it.

'Know this is its lot; it comes to death of its own will, and from death it comes to life. Hear what it signifies. Phoenix signifies Jesus, Son of Mary, that he had power to die of his own will, and from death came to life. Phoenix signifies that to save His people He chose to suffer upon the Cross.'

The glutton Emperor Heliogabalus (A.D. 218-222), who thought he had eaten every known dainty, one day remembered the phoenix, and determined, though there was only one, to have it killed and sent to him. Among the many birds of all kinds sent from the far corners of the empire came a Bird of Paradise, which was near enough the alleged likeness of the bird to be accepted.

In China the bird is the symbol of imperial authority, and its colours, given as being red, azure, yellow, white and black, represent their cardinal virtues of uprightness, humanity, virtue, honesty and sincerity, respectively. Its appearance was said to precede the advent of virtuous rulers.

However other strange birds may puzzle us, this one presents no difficulty. It originated from Heliopolis in Egypt, which town, as its name suggests, was the centre of the cult of sun worship. There was never a clearer sun symbol. Its colour, place of origin, and the direction from which it appeared—Arabia is due east of Egypt—combined with its faculty for resurrection, all point to the same explanation. The whole story was probably a parable for the common people made up by the sun priests at Heliopolis to explain their solar cycle.

The roc (opposite) and the phoenix (above) are among the host of fabulous birds inhabiting the aviary of mythology. A roc once rescued Sinbad the Sailor from an island, but here two rocs bombard Sinbad's ship with gigantic boulders to punish the sailors who had broken one of their eggs. Less worldly, the phoenix, which every 500 or so years resurrects itself from its nest of ashes, is associated with immortality.

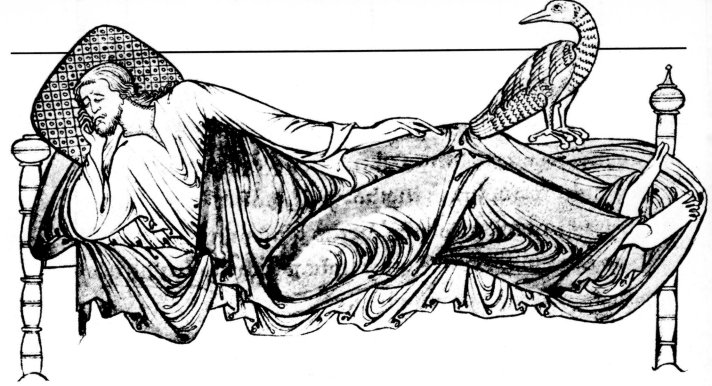

The Caladrius

For man to point the moral from the lower orders of creation has been the fashion from La Fontaine and John Gay back to Aesop's time, and doubtless long enough before. And not the least skilful were the monks of the Middle Ages, who used as propaganda the works of the Lord together with the imagination of man. There are extant several of their works, known as Bestiaries. These are a collection of beasts, birds, and reptiles, some real and some fabulous; the whole, with a minimum of accuracy and a maximum of fancy, beautifully illustrated and written. A short description of the subject is given, and then such improving moral analogies as the monks could think of are drawn, to be taken as powder with the jam.

One of the most beautiful of these Bestiaries is in the Bodleian Library at Oxford, and one of the birds described is the *Caladrius*. The following is a rendering of the Latin text.

'He is white with no black on him, and the inside of his thigh cures dimness in the eye. It is found in the palaces of kings. If anyone is in sickness, from this *Caladrius* it is known whether he will live or die. The sickness of the man is the sign that death is near. Soon the bird comes that he may see the sick man. If he turns his face from him, all may know that he is going to die. But if his sickness shall turn to health, he looks in his face, and takes within himself all the sickness of the man. He flies into the sky towards the sun, and burns and purges the sickness, and the patient is recovered.' Then morality gets the better of imagination, and the bird is likened to Christ, who was also without stain, and bore our sins aloft upon the Cross.

The Basilisk

Those who in these days experiment with the death ray may like to know that their idea, in legend at any rate, is some two or three thousand years old. The cockatrice, or basilisk, was a monster with the wings and head of a cock, and the tail of a dragon. 'He does not impel his body like other serpents', says Pliny, 'by a multiplied flexion, but advances lofty and upright. He kills the shrubs, not only by contact, but by breathing on them, and splits the rocks, such power of evil is there in him.' Another kind caused death by a glance merely. In Shakespeare's *Richard III*, when the King compliments Lady Anne on her eyes, she says 'Would they were basilisk's, to strike thee dead.'

The kind that killed by touch and not sight seem to have been charged with a sort of primitive electricity, for Lucan writes:

> What though the Moor the basilisk has slain
> And pinned him lifeless to the sandy plain;
> Up through the spear the subtle venom flies,
> The hand imbibes it, and the victor dies.

It was called Basiliskos, or king of serpents, partly because of its crest, and partly because all its subjects, whatever they might be doing, beat a respectful, if hasty, retreat when they heard it coming. The only plant that could withstand it was rue, and the weasel was supposed to eat the plant, and then attack the beast without fear or harm. The cockatrice was supposed to be hatched from an egg laid by a cock more than seven years old. This egg was incubated by a toad. In Basle, in 1474, a cock was formally tried, sentenced and executed for laying an egg. The popular rejoicing was great, as we could well understand if we believed as they did in the peril so hardly averted.

A stare from the caladrius (above) boded well for a sick person because the bird's favor meant the sufferer's convalescence. But woe to those upon whom the basilisk (right, as shown on a printer's logo in 1500) cast his eye, for his gaze brought death that could be averted only by the "venom" of a weasel or the crow of a cock. In regions where the basilisk was supposed to lurk, cautious travelers took cocks with them.

Below are gathered together the folklore of several birds, taken without regard to any logical connection between the species. They are in one company because they are not of sufficient importance to fly singly, and they are best described as by a sportsman writing up his game book at the end of the day — 'various.'

Swans

Stories of the swan are very common in Arian mythology, as all readers of Grimm and Hans Andersen will know. Freyr, the God of the Fruitful Land in Sweden and Iceland, was the Lord of Rain and Sunshine, and he travelled about in a chariot of white clouds named *Skibladnir*. Swans were sacred to him because, winging their way against a blue sky high above the earth, they represented the *cirri*, or fleecy white clouds in which he dwelt. The identification of the swan as a weather symbol has a parallel in Wales, where they used to say that the eggs were hatched by thunder and lightning.

In Classical myth is the story of Castor and Pollux, the twin sons of Leda, whom Zeus married in the shape of a swan. These heroes spent alternately one day among the Gods and the next upon earth; the story being a dramatization of the alternate rule in the heavens of the sun and the moon.

Another curious aspect of the swan in folklore is its connection with music. It was sacred to Apollo, the god of the Lyre; and the Egyptian hieroglyphic for music is a swan. Now the swan, normally, is anything but musical, though the clear strident note of its heavy wing-beats through the air may have seemed to early man to give it music wherever it went.

Plato, as well as Aristotle who was the first naturalist of his time, believed it. Modern evidence is conflicting, but whether it were a fact or not never bothered the poets, who found in it an image after their own heart. Shakespeare has many references to it and Tennyson wrote a very fine poem on the subject. And Byron, in *The Isles of Greece*, has the following verse:

> Place me on Sunium's marbled steep
> Where no one save the waves and I
> May hear our mutual murmurs sweep;
> There, swanlike, let me sing and die.

Effective in the hands of a master, this conceit has been worn threadbare by constant usage as representing any sort of death-bed speech or farewell. Perhaps Coleridge thought so too when he made that caustic epigram:

> Swans sing before they die: 'twere no bad thing
> Did some I wot of die before they sing.

Geese

We turn naturally to the swan's prosaic cousin, the goose. However homely the goose may be, it still lays golden eggs. The story is one of the most common, and there is scarcely a mythology without it in some

WHITE WAGTAILS

ENGLISH ROBIN

CROWS

SARUS CRANE

form or another. The Egyptians said that Seb, the father of Osiris, was a goose, and that this cosmic bird laid the sun as an egg. According to the Brahmins the Great Spirit laid a golden egg, which represents the sun, from which Brahma the Breath of Life was born.

The goose was sacred to Woden, probably in his capacity as god of storms, for it is the rough weather that drives the wild birds inland. It is still a common country expression when it snows to say that the Old Lady is plucking her geese.

Crows

We turn now to the smaller relations of the raven, the crows. They seem to have been all that the raven was, only, as befitted their size, in a less degree. The French peasants, for instance, say that whereas bad priests become ravens, bad nuns become crows. The Greeks disliked them, and their expression 'Go to the Crows' was the equivalent of our 'Go to Hell.' In Wales one was considered unlucky if a crow crossed his path, whereas

> Two crows I see
> Good luck to me.

One crow over a house means a death there within a year. They are exceedingly crafty birds, and the Roman expression 'to pierce a crow's eye' was the equivalent of the English 'catch a weasel asleep,' or practical impossibility.

Wagtails

It would be odd if so conspicuous a bird as the wagtail, which runs about the lawn beating time with its tail, had attracted no notice. The French peasants say that it had at one time no tail, but being asked to the lark's wedding, borrowed one from the wren, which is notoriously lacking in that respect. The bird took a fancy to the borrowed plumes and did not give them back, so that it is for ever wagging it to make sure that it is still there, and no one has stolen it.

Cranes

The crane is not a common bird, but is probably familiar enough. Cranes, when migrating, were supposed by the ancients to carry sand in their crop as ballast, and stones in their mouth to act as gags. These, when regurgitated, were supposed to be touchstones for gold. Further, when one of the flock was acting as sentry, with one leg bent up in the usual way, it was supposed to hold a stone in its claw, which would drop and arouse the bird in case it should doze. The 'crane in his vigilance' is always thus depicted in heraldry.

Birds of Paradise

Ornately plumed, gorgeously coloured, birds of paradise were the subject of an astounding set of nonsense. The birds were supposed to live on the scent of flowers and honey, and to flit for ever in the sun like spirits of

117

Paradise. They become drunk with the odour of nutmeg, fall to the ground, where the ants eat off their legs.

What actually happened was that in the 15th and 16th centuries when Portuguese traders found what a market there was for the birds' gorgeous plumes, they brought home the skins, having, naturally enough, cut off the unattractive legs. This gave rise to the widespread belief that the birds had none, and the consequent fables as to how they nested. Even so great a naturalist as Linnaeus named the birds *Paradisea apoda,* or 'footless.'

Swallows

The swallow has attracted a good deal of attention. The bird is much beloved in England and elsewhere, not so much because it is useful as well as harmless, but because, though one swallow does not make a summer, its arrival is a sure sign that summer is on the way. There was a swallow festival in ancient Greece in the spring. The Greek women used to catch a swallow if one found its way into a house, smear it with oil, and set it free to remove any ill luck. According to Aelian, the birds were sacred to the Household Gods. Nests on a house were supposed to bring luck, which would disappear if they were forsaken.

Although the swallow, generally speaking, was a lucky bird, there was the same inexplicable dual attitude towards it as towards the dove. German peasants hold that many swallows perching on a house spells poverty; the Celts disliked and feared the bird. If it flew beneath a man's arm or under a cow, then the man would lose the limb, and the cow would sicken and die.

English Robins

Last on the list because he is the first in our affections is the robin. He has always been the friend of man, frequented his home, and stayed with him during the sharpest winter. The bird goes unharmed now from motives of pure affection, but it was once sacred in the true sense. Its red breast marked it out as a bird sacred, even as the woodpecker was, to Thor, the Lightning god of the Norsemen. Penalties for harming it or its nest were that the home of the wrong doer would be destroyed by fire or lightning, or that the cows would give bloody milk.

We all know how the robin, for all his red breast, seeks shelter in barns and churches during cold weather. The two facts together have gone to make an old tale, originally Welsh. And we can leave the robin with a clear conscience when we have told it in Whittier's words.

> "Nay," said Grandmother, "have you not heard
> My poor bad boy, of the fiery pit,
> And how drop by drop this merciful bird
> Carries the water that quenches it?
> He brings cool dew in his little bill
> And lets it fall on the souls of men;
> You can see the marks on his red breast still
> Of the fires that scorch as he drops it in."

— W. J. Brown

Bird Watchers on Bird Watching

The Moment of Discovery...

John James Audubon

One incident of childhood is as perfect in my memory as if it had occurred this very day, and I have thought of it thousands of times since. It is one of the curious things which perhaps led me to love birds, and finally to study them with pleasure infinite. My foster mother had several beautiful parrots and some monkeys. One monkey was a full-grown male of a very large species. One morning, while the servants were engaged in arranging the room I was in, "Pretty Polly" asked for her breakfast as usual: "Mignonne wants bread and milk." The monkey, probably thinking the bird presumed upon his rights in the scale of Nature, walked deliberately towards her and, with unnatural composure, killed her. My infant heart agonized at this cruel sight. I prayed a servant to beat the monkey, but he refused because he preferred him to the parrot. My long and piercing cries brought my mother rushing into the room. I was tranquilized, the monkey forever afterward chained, and Mignonne buried with all the pomp of a cherished one.

As I grew up I was fervently desirous of becoming acquainted with Nature. But the moment a bird was dead, no matter how beautiful it had been in life, the pleasure of possession became blunted for me. I wished to possess all the productions of Nature, but I wished to see life in them, as fresh as from the hands of their Maker.

—1835

Julian Huxley

I had been fond of birds since a child; but it was when I was about fourteen that I became a real birdwatcher. The incident which precipitated the change was this. One morning of late winter, crossing the laundry-yard of my aunt's country house, I saw a green woodpecker on the grass only a few yards from me: I had just time to take in the sight of it before the bird was off to the wood beyond the hedge. The green woodpecker is a common bird enough; but I had never seen one close. Here I saw every striking detail: the rich green of the wings, the flash of bright yellow on the back when he flew, the pale glittering eye, the scarlet nape, the strange moustache of black and red; and the effect was as if I had seen a bird of paradise, even a phoenix. I was thrilled with the sudden realization that here, under my nose, in the familiar woods and fields, lived strange and beautiful creatures of whose strangeness and beauty I had been lamentably unaware.

—1930

John Burroughs

Years ago, when quite a youth, I was rambling in the woods one Sunday, with my brothers, gathering black birch, wintergreens, etc., when, as we reclined upon the ground, gazing vaguely up into the trees, I caught sight of a bird, that paused a moment on a branch above me, the like of which I had never before seen or heard of. It was probably the blue yellow-backed warbler, as I have since found this to be a common bird in those woods; but to my young fancy it seemed like some fairy bird, so curiously marked was it, and so new and unexpected. I saw it a moment as the flickering leaves parted, noted the white spot on its wing, and it was gone. How the thought of it clung to me afterward! It was a revelation. It was the first intimation I had had that the woods we knew so well held birds that we knew not at all. Were our eyes and ears so dull, then? There was the robin, the blue jay, the bluebird, the yellow-bird, the cherry-bird, the catbird, the chipping-bird, the woodpecker, the high-hole, an occasional redbird, and a few others, in the woods or along their borders, but who ever dreamed that there were still others that not even the hunters saw, and whose names no one had ever heard?

When, one summer day, later in life, I took my gun and went to the woods again, in a different though perhaps a less simple spirit, I found my youthful vision more than realized. There were, indeed, other birds, plenty of them, singing, nesting, breeding, among the familiar trees, which I had before passed by unheard and unseen.

It is a surprise that awaits every student of ornithology, and the thrill of delight that accompanies it, and the feeling of fresh, eager inquiry that follows, can hardly be awakened by any other pursuit. Take the first step in ornithology, procure one new specimen, and you are ticketed for the whole voyage. There is a fascination about it quite overpowering. It fits so well with other things, — with fishing, hunting, farming, walking, camping-out — with all that takes one to the fields and woods. One may go a blackberrying and make some rare discovery; or, while driving his cow to pasture, hear a new song, or make a new observation. Secrets lurk on all sides. There is news in every bush. Expectation is ever on tiptoe. What no man ever saw before may the next moment be revealed to you. What a new interest the woods have! How you long to explore every nook and corner of them! You would even find consolation in being lost in them. You could then hear the night birds

CATBIRD

WESTERN MEADOWLARK

GILDED FLICKER

CEDAR WAXWING

ROBIN

WOOD THRUSH

MYRTLE WARBLER

GREEN WOODPECKER

CHIPPING SPARROW

...A Lifetime of Rewards

and the owls, and, in your wanderings, might stumble upon some unknown specimen.

In all excursions to the woods or to the shore, the student of ornithology has an advantage over his companions. He has one more resource, one more avenue of delight. He, indeed, kills two birds with one stone and sometimes three. If others wander, he can never go out of his way. His game is everywhere. The cawing of a crow makes him feel at home, while a new note or a new song drowns all care. Audubon, on the desolate coast of Labrador, is happier than any king ever was; and on shipboard is nearly cured of his seasickness when a new gull appears in sight.

One must taste it to understand or appreciate its fascination. The looker-on sees nothing to inspire such enthusiasm. Only a little feathers and a half-musical note or two; why all this ado? "Who would give a hundred and twenty dollars to know about the birds?" said an Eastern governor, half contemptuously, to Wilson, as the latter solicited a subscription to his great work. Sure enough. Bought knowledge is dear at any price. The most precious things have no commercial value. It is not, your Excellency, mere technical knowledge of the birds that you are asked to purchase, but a new interest in the fields and woods, a new moral and intellectual tonic, a new key to the treasure-house of nature. Think of the many other things your Excellency would get, — the air, the sunshine, the healing fragrance and coolness, and the many respites from the knavery and turmoil of political life.

————————————————————— 1899

BLACK-THROATED BLUE WARBLER (BURROUGHS'S "BLUE YELLOW-BACKED WARBLER")

EASTERN MEADOWLARK

Julian Huxley

One of the bird-watcher's most obvious rewards is that the countryside soon becomes alive to him in a new way. Every kind of bird has its own particular quality or character, so to speak, which derives partly from its size and colouring and voice, partly from its temperament and habits, partly from the surroundings where one is accustomed to see it.

To go out on a country walk and see and hear different kinds of wild birds is thus to the bird-watcher rather like running across a number of familiar neighbours, local characters, or old acquaintances. The walk becomes a series of personal encounters instead of a mere walk. A correspondent sends me the following quotation (whose author I have been unable to discover) which beautifully sums up what I mean: 'He whose ear is untaught to enjoy the harmonious discord of the birds, travels alone when he might have company.'

————————————————————— 1930

Louis J. Halle

The appreciation of warblers is a slow acquisition, since most of the species are to be seen and heard only for a few days each year, and the rarer may be seen only at intervals of several years. When I say that I have been acquainted with a warbler for ten years, it may be that the sum of that acquaintance is only a few minutes. Perhaps I have seen the bird and heard its song only a half-dozen times, and then when I was distracted by the presence of its innumerable congeners. The appreciation of birds, indeed the appreciation of all the phenomena of spring, cannot be dissociated from the accumulations of memory. The appearance of a familiar bird immediately awakens a train of forgotten associations, and this makes each spring transcend its predecessor. The interest accumulates and is compounded. The first yellow-throated warbler next year will be the

126

more meaningful to me as it brings back that moment in the woods opposite Dyke. For one remembers clearly enough the fact of such a moment, but only an evocative sight or sound or smell can bring back the full emotion. The person who sees the bird for the first time cannot know what moves me. . . . One must share common memories in order to share common experiences.

——————————————————————— **1947**

Theodore Roosevelt

I spoke about the sweet singing of the Western meadow lark and plains skylark; neither of them kin to the true skylark, by the way, one being a cousin of the grackles and hangbirds, and the other a kind of pipit. To me both of these birds are among the most attractive singers to which I have ever listened, but of all bird music much must be allowed for the surroundings and much for the mood and the keenness of sense of the listener. The lilt of the little plains skylark is neither powerful nor very melodious, but it is sweet, pure, long sustained, with a ring of courage befitting a song uttered in high air.

The meadow lark is a singer of a higher order, deserving to rank with the best. Its song has length, variety, power, and rich melody and there is in it sometimes a cadence of wild sadness, inexpressibly touching. Yet I cannot say that either song would appeal to others as it appeals to me, for to me it comes forever laden with a hundred memories and associations, with the sight of dim hills reddening in the dawn, with the breath of cool morning winds blowing across lonely plains, with the scent of flowers on the sunlit prairie, with the motion of fiery horses, with the strong thrill of eager and buoyant life.

——————————————————————**1893**

Henry David Thoreau

On the 29th of April, as I was fishing from the bank of the river near the Nine-Acre-Corner bridge, standing on the quaking grass and willow roots, where the muskrats lurk, I heard a singular rattling sound, somewhat like that of the sticks which boys play with their fingers, when, looking up, I observed a very slight and graceful hawk, like a nighthawk, alternately soaring like a ripple and tumbling a rod or two over and over, showing the under side of its wings, which gleamed like a satin ribbon in the sun, or like the pearly inside of a shell. This sight reminded me of falconry and what nobleness and poetry are associated with that sport. The merlin it seemed

AMERICAN BITTERN

to me it might be called: but I care not for its name. It was the most ethereal flight I had ever witnessed. It did not simply flutter like a butterfly, nor soar like the larger hawks, but it sported with proud reliance in the fields of air; mounting again and again with its strange chuckle, it repeated its free and beautiful fall, turning over and over like a kite, and then recovering from its lofty tumbling, as if it had never set its foot on *terra firma*. It appeared to have no companion in the universe,—sporting there alone,—and to need none but the morning and the ether with which it played. It was not lonely, but made all the earth lonely beneath it. Where was the parent which hatched it, its kindred, and its father in the heavens? The tenant of the air, it seemed related to the earth but by an egg hatched some time in the crevice of a crag;—or was its native nest made in the angle of a cloud, woven of the rainbow's trimmings and the sunset sky, and lined with some soft midsummer haze caught up from earth? Its eyry now some cliffy cloud.

Beside this I got a rare mess of golden and silver and bright cupreous fishes, which looked like a string of jewels. Ah! I have penetrated to those meadows on the morning of many a first spring day, jumping from hummock to hummock, from willow root to willow root, when the wild river valley and the woods were bathed in so pure and bright a light as would have waked the dead, if they had been slumbering in their graves as some suppose. There needs no stronger proof of immortality. All things must live in such a light. O Death, where was thy sting? O Grave, where was thy victory, then?

Our village life would stagnate if it were not for the unexplored forests and meadows which surround it. We need the tonic of wilderness,—to wade sometimes in marshes where the bittern and the meadow-hen lurk, and hear the booming of the snipe; to smell the whispering sedge where only some wilder and more solitary fowl builds her nest, and the mink crawls with its belly close to the ground. At the same time that we are earnest to explore and learn all things, we require that all things be mysterious and unexplorable, that land and sea be infinitely wild, unsurveyed and unfathomed by us because unfathomable. We can never have enough of nature. We must be refreshed by the sight of inexhaustible vigor, vast and titanic features, the sea-coast with its wrecks, the wilderness with its living and its decaying trees, the thunder-cloud, and the rain which lasts three weeks and produces freshets. We need to witness our own limits transgressed, and some life pasturing freely where we never wander.

Birds Among the Skyscrapers

Thousands of birds over Manhattan's desert of skyscrapers at daybreak! Most people are sleeping too soundly at that hour to be aware of the faint chips, chirps and lisps that shower from the dim but lightening sky. The heart of New York City is hardly the place where one would expect to find large numbers of migrating wanderers. Chicago has its Lincoln Park, and Boston its Public Gardens, but New York boasts the most famous birdtrap of all—Central Park. This two and one-half mile long park, set like a narrow oblong emerald among Gotham's towers, is, at times, an amazing place for birds. More than 220 species have been recorded there.

Most small birds migrate at night. Clear, warm nights in late April or early May are best, evenings with a gentle breeze from the southwest, especially after a spell of poor weather. These are the nights when the small travelers by the hundreds of thousands sweep northward up the globe, unseen. When dawn approaches they drop into the trees nearest at hand. But imagine the predicament of those following the northeastern flyway, when they reach this metropolitan area at daybreak!

What a discouraging outlook for a small, tired bird! By the weak eastern light nothing can be discerned but a vast arid jumble of steel and stone, cut by sterile gorges and steep canyons. In the distance a blur of green becomes dimly visible—Central Park. Some nearly exhausted birds may drop down to the few bushes in Washington Square or even to a scraggly ailanthus in a Greenwich Village courtyard, but most of them struggle on until they reach the more promising oasis of the park.

The park policeman pounding his beat and the homeless unfortunate sprawling on a bench are not the only humans astir at that hour. There are the bird watchers, too; and if it is the month of May, scores of them. To appreciate the force of the attraction, you need only to drape yourself on the rail of the bridge at the head of the park lake on a May dawn. The calls of the birds shower out of the purplish half-light, weakly and from a great height, at first; but as visibility increases the birds drop lower, and an occasional dim form can be seen pitching into the nearest trees. During the minutes that follow, the chorus of song gradually swells until the voices of scores of birds are blended to greet the

To a passing bird, Central Park (opposite) looms out of the concrete landscape like a waterhole in a desert. The birds on the following four pages are but a few of the hundreds of species seen at various times of the year in the park. Some birds, like the house sparrow on page 133, establish residences among the towering buildings of Manhattan.

morning sun as it rises and glows from the direction of Fifth Avenue.

The biggest concentration point is "the Ramble," two verdant acres threaded by winding paths and a trickling stream between 72nd and 77th Streets, near the American Museum of Natural History. Being more remote from the main automobile boulevards and with a heavier growth of trees, it is the logical place for a bird to wander into.

Many bird watchers take a turn or two about the Ramble before office hours. Others, less determined, wander in at nine or ten o'clock. These miss half the fun. The binocular is the badge of their brotherhood and anyone with a pair can be confidently approached on a basis of friendship. "Birdmen" (airmen are really "manbirds") are as gregarious as the flocks they follow, although some find more pleasure in foraging alone.

A few years ago a prothonotary warbler, a bird of southern swamps, with burnished gold head and breast, put in an appearance. It remained for days and could always be located by the large ring of admirers surrounding it. Their unabashed enthusiasm had its effect on some of the casual strollers. Because of that one golden bird a number of people took up the study of birds.

The record for Central Park is seventy-nine species in one day. Surely an eightieth must have been around somewhere. A blanket of fog hanging low over the city that dawn had confused a horde of birds that would otherwise have gained Van Cortlandt Park or the woods of Westchester County. Early in the morning, when I left my lodgings in Brooklyn, I could hear and see many small birds flying low in the fog, barely clearing the tops of the buildings. Late that afternoon, after my classes at the Art Student's League, I hurried to the park to find it jammed with birds—not only in the Ramble, but from 59th Street all the way to the north end of the park. At 110th Street, where they had been stopped in their tree-to-tree wanderings by the forbidding wall of buildings, the branches buzzed with birds. Overawed, the bewildered observers could only look about and gasp. Imagine half a dozen vivid scarlet tanagers in a single tree and four smart-looking rose-breasted grosbeaks in another! In the row of bushes outside the old Casino, now torn down, I saw all five species of brown thrushes. Even the woodcock, that long-nosed recluse, was there.

One day an excited woman reported a chicken-sized bird with a purple breast, greenish wings, yellow legs and a red and blue bill. It swam, and climbed along the

STARLINGS

branches of the willow trees, she said. Investigation proved her fantastic description to be absolutely correct. It was a purple gallinule, a bird of the southern rice fields and swamps—the first one recorded in New York State in forty-nine years. We were so excited when we heard about it at the Linnaean meeting that the whole Bronx County Bird Club hurried up to the 110th Street lake, even though it was eleven o'clock at night. We saw the bird silhouetted against the reflections of Harlem's street light on the water, pumping its head as it swam, in typical gallinule fashion.

Not every day is a good bird watching day in Central Park, however. On some mornings the Ramble is almost birdless. Migrants seem to come in "waves." The migration watchers study the high and low pressure areas on the weather maps and try to predict these waves.

During the summer, little more than starlings, grackles, flickers, sparrows and robins can be found in the park. Winter is dull, too, but sometimes an unusual bird strays in. For two winters a barred owl perched every day in the same tree above a squirrel box, near 77th Street. It became one of the sights of Fifth Avenue and bus conductors pointed it out to their passengers.

My best find in winter was among the ducks on the 59th Street lake. In an ice-free patch of water, roped off from skaters, several hundred wild black ducks gather to share the food thrown to the swans and tame mallards. Sometimes a wild baldpate, pintail or shoveller drops in, creating a striking picture of wildlife against the towering skyline dominated by the Sherry-Netherland Hotel. One January day I noted a strange new duck, something like a mallard, but grayer, with a green crown and tan cheeks. I passed it by as one of the innumerable domestic hybrids that mingle with the wild birds on the pond. Later, I realized this was the same duck which Audubon had painted and which he called the bemaculated or Brewer's duck. Audubon had picked up a specimen that had been shot somewhere in Louisiana, and what he had was a hybrid between the mallard and the gadwall. The bird on the 59th Street pond was Audubon's "bemaculated duck," feather for feather, a hybrid so rare that there is not a single specimen in the vast collection of *Anatidae* in the American Museum of Natural History.

Strange birds, escaped from zoos, pet shops and aviaries, sometimes roam the park. Brazilian cardinals, waxbills and even parrots have been seen. A few years ago a European chaffinch spent the winter amicably with a flock of English sparrows. One day a curator at the American Museum came across a bewildered group of birders staring goggle-eyed at a pied hornbill from India! On another occasion Allan Cruickshank rushed into my office and announced excitedly that a strange duck had dropped into the small lake behind the Art Museum. In all his twenty years of birding he had never seen anything like it. Together we hurried to the pond. The "duck," which puzzled us both for awhile, turned out to be a maned goose from Australia, free flying, but obviously an "escape."

Birds turn up in odd spots all over the crowded island of Manhattan. Guy Emerson, Edson Heck and other residents of Greenwich Village, have made surprising lists of birds around their homes where hardly anything but a ginkgo or an ailanthus tree will grow. One November there was an invasion of dovekies, the little auk that usually spends the winter far at sea. Easterly gales had forced them inland and several were found swimming in rain-flooded gutters. I have seen a barred owl in a tree outside the City Hall, a tiny saw-whet owl on Riverside Drive, a great blue heron flying down Fifth Avenue and a flock of curlew over Greenwich Village.

At least a dozen peregrine falcons spend the winter each year among the towers of Greater New York, taking tribute from the flocks of fat lazy pigeons that befoul the ledges. One winter, a young red-tailed hawk spent two or three months around the Metropolitan Museum, perching above the ornate facade, where I could watch it from my office window across the street.

On some misty evenings hundreds of small birds can be seen fluttering through the brilliant lights that illuminate the tall towers of Radio City. During spring and fall, many birds come to the Gardens of the Nations high up on this modern Tower of Babel. On autumn nights, when the wind is in the northwest, I sometimes take the elevator to the observation platform, sixty-odd stories above the street. There, far below, the city lights are strung like jewels to the hazy horizon, while close about me in the blackness I can hear the small voices of southbound migrants. For a few brief moments I feel as if I were one of them.

On a warm fall day several years ago a southward-bound hermit thrush, weary of picking its way through the bewildering canyons of New York, descended to the sidewalk on Madison Avenue at the southeast corner of 63rd Street. The display of palms and flowers in the shop of Christatos & Koster must have suggested to the thrush its tropical destination, and it flew in through the open transom, taking refuge in a secluded corner.

All through the winter the bird led a happy existence and finally became so tame it would alight on anyone's hand to secure a meal worm. Marco, as he was christened for no accountable reason, had many admirers who used to drop in to pay their respects. The following spring he was restless and one day, when the transom windows were open, he departed. His friends hoped that he had gotten safely out of New York and joined his fellow hermit thrushes in their flight to the northern woods.

The small songbirds, like Marco, that become entrapped by the metropolis, cannot be called normal residents. They are not like the ever-present gulls that have adapted their ecology to the cities along the coasts and the Great Lakes. At any time of day gulls may be seen floating over New York's skyscrapers—herring gulls in winter, laughing gulls in summer—trading between the East River and the Hudson—or merely flying over Central Park to the 86th Street reservoir to take a fresh-water bath.

The very best spot for gulls is the sewer outlet at 92nd Street in Brooklyn. For several years now the little gull

PURPLE MARTINS

HOUSE SPARROW

GULL AT A CAFE TABLE

ROBIN

(*Larus minutus*), a tiny European species with smoky-black wing linings, has been seen with the buoyant Bonaparte's gulls, snatching tidbits that well up in the sordid flow. Here in the Narrows, where immigrants get their first view of the Statue of Liberty, I have seen both this and another European, the black-headed gull. Curiously enough, the only other place on our whole Atlantic coast where these two rare *Laridae* from the other side can be depended on is also at a sewer outlet, at Newburyport, Massachusetts.

It is a standing jest among bird watchers along the coast that there is no place like a good garbage dump for birds. Among my favorite sites in years past have been the dumps at Dyker Heights in Brooklyn, at Newark Bay and at Hunt's Point in the Bronx. There have been others, too, but these in particular bring fond, though odoriferous memories. During one of their cyclic eruptions there were four snowy owls at the Hunt's Point dump. Some might say they frequented the place for concealment because they resembled packages of garbage wrapped in newspaper—white with black print—but a more likely reason was the abundance of rats. One winter we had twelve short-eared owls in the marsh adjacent to this dump and that, mind you, was deep inside metropolitan New York, along the bustling East River, with apartment houses crowding on all sides.

Leonard Dubkin, in his *Murmur of Wings*, has shown that even where the heavy hand of urbanization has locked the green world into a sarcophagus of cement and stone, there are opportunities to watch birds—even if only house sparrows or starlings. But most cities compromise with nature a little more than New York and Chicago do. Washington, D.C., is virtually a city in the woods. John Burroughs wrote of it in *Wake Robin*: "There is perhaps not another city in the Union that has on its very threshold so much natural beauty and grandeur such as men seek for in the remote forests and mountains." Theodore Roosevelt, during his term of office in Washington, made a list of birds he saw on the White House grounds. If anything, there are more birds in the nation's capital now than when these men lived there. Burroughs spoke of the cardinal as a shy bird—an uncommon sight. And the mockingbird was almost unknown in Washington then. Now both can be found in the very heart of town.

I feel certain that as our cities grow older they will harbor more birds, not fewer. As the newness and rawness wear off, species after species that has fled the carpenter and the mason will return to find their niches in the aging trees and gardens, just as the birds in the Old World cities have done.

— Roger Tory Peterson

Dashing scarlet tanagers (above) and purple gallinules (right) are both visitors to Central Park, though the gallinule only rarely wanders that far away from its southern swampland haunts.

On the Wings
of a Bird

Lying in bed early one cool March morning, before the hush that hung over the sleeping city had been broken by the first of the noises that the young day would bring, I saw a compact black body shoot with the speed of a comet across the square of blue sky framed like a picture in the open window. In an instant I was on my feet; and in another instant, I was leaning far out across the sill. Yonder it was, a hundred feet above the wet, glistening roofs to the northwest, cleaving the still, fresh air like some aerial torpedo. I gazed at it until it was gone, and doubtless my disappointment was written large upon my sleepy face. After all, it was only a loon—and I had hoped to see a wild goose!

Only a loon, bound, perhaps, for some cold glassy lake within the Arctic Circle—only a Great Northern Diver, answering the call of the North. What was a loon that it should lure a sane man from his warm bed two hours too soon on a chilly morning in March? I asked myself the question as I stood by the window, looking across my neighbor's lot at the houses beyond. A cardinal, half-hidden in the vivid new foliage of a sugarberry tree, glowed in the sunlight like a great drop of blood; and on a tall chimney farther away a slim gray mockingbird sang of the joys that April never failed to bring. Overhead, nineteen black vultures passed in procession, coming into town from their sleeping place across the river. A large flock of satiny waxwings lisping monotonously and all at once, settled among the branches of the sugarberry where the cardinal perched; and in the brown grasses beneath the window half a dozen white-throated sparrows searched industriously for breakfast.

My gaze roved from cardinal to mockingbird, from waxwing to sparrow; and my thoughts rushed northward with the vanished loon. And then, of a sudden, the old wonder that had thrilled me so often as I stood by that west window or under the garden elms. What if the loon were a common bird on the river in winter? It was, nevertheless, one of the wildest of the wild things; and from the window overlooking my garden in the midst of one of the oldest parts of the old city of Charleston, South Carolina, I had seen it!

My garden has few flowers in it. It is not really a garden at all, but a small and unkempt green place of trees, shrubbery, canes, and grass. Birds do not care for flowers. They prefer vine-tangles and weeds, thickets and trees; and I am more interested in birds than in roses. Watching these birds of my garden at odd moments between working hours, I have learned things that I might never have learned in the woods; yet I have learned only a very small part of what there is to learn about the wild life of this small city lot. Scarcely a month passes that does not teach something new, and now and again there comes some great surprise. Not long ago, I looked out of a window one morning and saw in one of the sugarberry trees behind the kitchen a bird that no one, so far as is known, had ever seen in a Charleston garden before. It was a yellow-crowned night heron, in the dark-brown, white-spotted plumage that every bird of that species wears during the first year or so of its life—a yellow-crowned night heron within fifty feet of my bedroom window!

That was a red-letter day; for although the yellow-crowned heron breeds along this coast, it is one of the shyest of its tribe, and you must go to the deep swamps or lonely marshes far from the homes of men if you would see it.

It is pleasant to recall some of the other great surprises—some of the other red-letter days in the history of the garden, each one of them rendered unforgettable by the coming of some unlooked-for feathered stranger. Such a day was that third of May when I looked up from my book to find a male scarlet tanager in the elm sapling beside the piazza. So rare is this bird in the lowlands of South Carolina that at the time when I saw this tanager there were only two other authentic records of the occurrence of the species in this region. Another day that will not soon be forgotten was a fourteenth of February when a woodcock stood on the top of a flat stump not twenty feet from the piazza. Since then I have learned to look for woodcocks in the garden in very cold weather and I have seen them there many times. There was an October morning which was made memorable by the arrival of two visitors from the North, of a species that few observers have ever seen on this coast—a pair of red-breasted nuthatches; while April 18, 1909, will stand always among the greatest of the great days of the garden, because on that morning I found in my elms a band of eight or ten pine siskins—a bird almost if not quite as rare in this part of the world as the scarlet tanager.

After all, however, it is not in the chance visit of some rare member of the feathered tribes that the charm of garden ornithology chiefly lies. For me, the fascination

---

Herbert Ravenel Sass exulted in the endless pageantry of birds that visited the luxuriant tangle of "trees, shrubbery, canes, and grass" growing in his garden in Charleston, S.C. Some of the birds he saw— common and uncommon—are shown on the following two pages.

of the study—or diversion, as I should more modestly call it—is found, first in the wonderful fact that even here amid the streets and houses of a modern city I see from time to time—in some cases, regularly each year—some of the feathered people that are thought to be most fearful of man and most characteristic of the wilderness; and second, in the continued presence, throughout the year, or during certain periods, of other birds, common and familiar, perhaps, and known by name to every country boy, yet possessing and sometimes betraying secrets that cannot be learned from the books of the wisest of those who have gone before us.

There is a sequestered corner of the garden where a few tall elms and bushy privet trees cast so dark a shade that even in midsummer the moist black soil is bare of weeds and grass. Here, in April, August, and September, I see the hooded warbler, resplendent in yellow and sable, gleaning to the good things to be found in the thick foliage. Hither in April and August comes the gorgeous prothonotary, whose flame-coloured breast

GARDEN AT THE SASS HOME

is like a fragment of glowing cloud stolen from an autumn sunset and whose song rings just as clear and bold here amid the houses as in the sombre swamps that I must penetrate to find him when I go bird-hunting elsewhere than in the garden.

The clump of fig bushes hiding the angle formed by the fence and the back of a neighbour's outbuilding seems to possess a strange attraction for the sedate black and white warblers that visit it in spring and autumn; and it was in these same bushes that I saw the only black and white warbler ever seen by any man—so far as is known to science—in South Carolina in the month of December. When the first cool wave of autumn freshens the sultry air of September, many redstarts—with most of the red washed out of them—wage war on the slender pale-green larvae that hide, all in vain, under the small saw-edged leaves of the terminal twiglets of the elms. In April, September, and October

I sometimes see the handsome black-throated blue warbler, solemn with a most unwarblerlike solemnity, moving in silence from branch to branch where the shadow is darkest; while the parula, the prairie warbler, the summer yellow-bird, and, in the depth of winter, the hardy little yellow-rump, are among the other warblers that are more or less familiar visitors to the spot.

From the vague dome-like mass of a fig tree near the piazza—a darker shadow among dark shadows—comes a clear flute-like whistle repeated again and again. It is a cardinal singing in the gloom—singing perhaps to the yellow moon that peeps now and then from behind the scurrying drifts of cloud. I am ashamed. I have written page after page about the birds of my garden and scarcely a word have I written about those that should occupy the most exalted place. Tempted by the unusual, I have ignored the ordinary, which in all our affairs is generally the most important. I have passed over those more familiar birds that are most characteristic of the place. I do not know what the garden would be like if its cardinals and its mockingbirds were taken away. In sunshine and in rain, in summer and in winter, they are my comrades, these two. Better than the weather god himself, the red-coated cardinal knows when spring is coming: but he does not wait for spring, and I have heard him singing his bold, free song outside my window on Christmas morning. He is the guardian spirit of the garden, my honest handsome Redcoat; and for him and his fair gentle-mannered wife a goodly portion of cracked corn is placed each day on the feeding stump under the graceful elm in which, when it was a slender sapling, I saw the scarlet tanager.

The mockingbird's character is not without its defects; he strays now and then from the strait path of rectitude that Redcoat follows faithfully to the end of his days. The mockingbird is one of the bravest creatures that breathe the air. He will venture his life in defense of his nest, and I have seen him actually put a fair-sized dog to flight; but often have I heaped abuse upon his head because in utterly causeless fury he has smitten hip and thigh some unusual visitor to the garden; and as often have I granted him forgiveness of his sin when, after routing the inoffensive object of his wrath, he has mounted light as air to the topmost twig of the willow and, perching there, has poured forth to the calm sky above such music as no other bird can make.

In the drawer of my desk is the unfinished manuscript of a history of the garden's birds—dry, concise (I hope), and matter-of-fact, treating each species separately and in order; but, of the people that I know, many would judge its author a fool for spending precious moments in work so barren of material profit. Yet in this little green place amid the city's houses there is matter for a century of study. Within the boundaries of these fences I have learned a few things that have been worth learning, and I have discovered there something of what Hudson calls "the wonderfulness and eternal mystery of life itself."

Herbert Ravenel Sass

PARULA WARBLERS

HOODED WARBLER

BLACK-AND-WHITE WARBLER

PROTHONOTARY WARBLERS

WHITE-THROATED SPARROW

PRAIRIE WARBLER

CARDINAL

RED-BREASTED NUTHATCH

YELLOW-CROWNED NIGHT HERON

PINE SISKIN

Have You Started Your Life List?

It was 15 years ago that my husband Red upset our lives. He bought me binoculars and Roger Tory Peterson's *A Field Guide to the Birds of Texas.* I aimed the binoculars at a bird pecking a hole in a tree, and in sudden, unbelieving awe gasped, "He's so beautiful!" Flipping through Peterson, I found my bird was a red-bellied woodpecker, no question about it.

From that moment, without even leaving home, I became a great discoverer. An anonymous brownish wisp became a jaunty Bewick's wren delivering song wholesale. A pair of Carolina chickadees taught me birds can be tender. I discovered neighbors I had never met — comical, richly colored green herons.

I didn't realize it, but I had a galloping case of birding fever. Red, too. Eventually our enthusiasm led Red into a wildlife filming career and me into writing a syndicated column about birds.

Unknown to us at the time, hundreds of others were happily discovering birds. A survey issued in 1965 by the U.S. Census Bureau showed that "hunters" carrying binoculars and cameras had become almost as numerous as those carrying guns. Today the wave of interest rolls on. Roger Peterson, world renowned bird artist and bird guide author, estimates the birding clan has grown ten-fold in the last ten years or so, and his field guides have sold more than two million copies in American editions alone.

The appeal of birding is as diverse as the people who play it. Psychologist James A. Tucker of Austin, Texas, coordinator for the American Birding Association, analyzes: "Birding is a modern way of matching one's self against the elements." Alex Griesman, Angwin, California, painting contractor, feels that birding reveals the diversity of God, not just in birds, but in everything around us.

Nature seminars, nature camps, bird identification classes, and resorts that cater to birding and nature buffs are increasing. Guided birding tours now visit nearly every spot on earth. It is estimated that the famous whooping cranes bring at least one million tourist dollars to Texas annually. In some localities special telephones give recorded information on the latest local bird finds, and bird lists are included with tourist information from chambers of commerce.

Along with this interest has come a game officially called "birding," with a membership that is estimated to have multiplied 100-fold in the last ten years. The game started in the United States, but has spread to a score of other countries on five continents.

The goal of birding is to find and identify different species of birds in order to tally them as a score. There are, for example, about 700 species of wild birds in America north of Mexico. The first to identify that number in this territory was Joseph W. Taylor, a retired corporation officer of Honeoye Falls, New York. Taylor trudged, cold and wet, an average of nine miles a day over the inhospitable tundra and glacial rocks of Attu Island in Alaska to complete his record. Asian and Pacific birds sometimes stray to this westernmost point of North America, and Taylor's 700th bird was just such an occasional wanderer, a gray-spotted flycatcher, the only member of its family ever seen on this continent.

To count in a birder's score, a new bird must be wild, unrestrained and alive, must be correctly identified by the player himself, and must be seen in a "designated territory." A designated territory includes whatever area the individual player chooses. But whether it's an invalid's backyard or a continent, once it has been decided upon, its boundaries must be strictly adhered to. When a birder positively identifies a bird species for the first time *within this territory,* he gets to add one point to his list (or score) for that territory.

Such scores listed for states or provinces, nations, continents, or the world are in direct competition with the scores of other birders scouting the same territories. The American Birding Association is the official recorder of all such scores.

G. Stuart Keith, a British ornithologist on the staff of New York's American Museum of Natural History, and first president of the American Birding Association, is unquestionably the present champion birder of the world. For 26 years Keith has stalked birds in 40 countries on every continent. He has identified 5,000 species of birds — more than half of the earth's known species.

Ted Parker, III, set a record in 1971 for the number of species identified in North America north of Mexico in a single year by one person. A Lancaster, Pennsylvania, high school senior at the time, he learned where different kinds of birds were most likely to be found, then set up a complicated schedule for weekends and school vacations that would take him to the best spots during the best time. At the end of his year-long pursuit, Ted had piled up a spectacular North American annual list record of 626 species.

Kenn Kaufman of Wichita, Kansas, has proved that almost any determined birder can join the competition. Kenn began birding at the age of six and dug dandelions from neighbors' lawns to earn $20 for his first pair of binoculars at age ten. In 1973, 19-year-old Kenn gathered his necessities in a heavy backpack and started over the country to break Ted Parker's North American annual record. Camping out along the way and spending almost nothing, Kenn identified 671 birds, shattering Parker's 626 record.

Though there is glory and excitement in champion birding, the lasting contributions of the sport may come from "locality" birders like Mary Anne McClendon, who has faithfully studied her Austin, Texas, area for years. Her remarkable record of 320 species observed in Travis County alone, when added to those of similar observers across the nation, form a massive body of scientific information. Both private and government organizations use lay volunteers in a wide range of studies. Such bird data on declining numbers, disease and malformations may serve as an early warning system against environmental deteriorations.

Why do birders bird? "Why does a man climb a mountain?" parries G. Stuart Keith, the champion birder.

Birds do many of the things humans do, as we may see ourselves mirrored in some of their habits and actions. They can be comical, tragic, joyous, tender, fierce or puzzling, matching almost any basic human behavior. And birding can change the way we see our surroundings. When Red and I drove from Texas to the famous prairie pothole nesting country of North Dakota where thousands of birds raise their young each summer, we tallied by states the birds we were able to identify, starting a new list of species at each state line. The hundreds of miles of midwestern croplands, prairies and semi-deserts, which easily could have become boring, instead were exciting.

Further, birding can be played almost anywhere, in any season, by anyone. While it grows constantly harder to find a place to hunt or fish, birds can be viewed just outside our windows. Though deserts and marshes have their special kinds of birds, so do barnyards and garbage dumps.

Since birding has no referee or judge, how can one know that everyone is playing honestly? The answer is that even in simple, day-to-day birding, a player's level of competence and self-discipline can't be hidden. Any birder who reports species he is never able to show his fellow birders soon destroys his own credibility. Rare sightings are seldom officially accepted unless they are confirmed by competent observers.

So much of birding's pleasure comes from showing discoveries to someone else that there are few players who are "loners." In fact, Jim Tucker thinks, "Birding is creating a new form of competition—a rivalry to see who can help the other guy the most! The real test is based more and more on mutual aid rather than on trying to knock the other fellow down."

Birds, with their mobility, grace and beauty, are a constant symbol of freedom. Watching them, we humans begin to understand that we are governed by the same laws of nature. We begin to fathom our frightening power over living beings. A larger philosophy is born when we comprehend that misuse of this power may decide not only the fate of other life, but of our own as well.

— **Marjorie Valentine Adams**

Up from the Egg: The Confessions of a Nuthatch Avoider

Bird watchers top my honors list.
I aimed to be one, but I missed.
Since I'm both myopic and astigmatic,
My aim turned out to be erratic,
And I, bespectacled and binocular,
Exposed myself to comment jocular.
We don't need too much birdlore, do we,
To tell a flamingo from a towhee;
Yet I cannot, and never will,
Unless the silly bird stands still.
And there's no enlightenment in a tour
Of ornithological literature.
Is yon strange creature a common chickadee,
Or a migrant alouette from Picardy?
You rush to consult your Nature guide
And inspect the gallery inside,
But a bird in the open never looks
Like its picture in the birdie books—
Or if it once did, it has changed its plumage,
And plunges you back into ignorant gloomage.
That is why I sit here growing old by inches,
Watching the clock instead of finches,
But I sometimes visualize in my gin
The Audubon that I audibin.

OGDEN NASH

Sharing a Shrinking Planet

Glimpsing the _Darkness_

Theodore Roosevelt

The western-most island we visited [in the Mississippi Sound] was outside the national reservation, and that very morning it had been visited and plundered by a party of eggers. The eggs had been completely cleared from most of the island, gulls and terns had been shot, and the survivors were in a frantic state of excitement. It was a good object-lesson in the need of having reserves, and laws protecting wild life, and a sufficient number of efficient officers to enforce the laws and protect the reserves. Defenders of the short-sighted men who in their greed and selfishness will, if permitted, rob our country of half its charm by their reckless extermination of all useful and beautiful wild things sometimes seek to champion them by saying that "the game belongs to the people." So it does; and not merely to the people now alive, but to the unborn people. The "greatest good of the greatest number" applies to the number within the womb of time, compared to which those now alive form but an insignificant fraction. Our duty to the whole, including the unborn generations, bids us restrain an unprincipled present-day minority from wasting the heritage of these unborn generations. The movement for the conservation of wild life, and the larger movement for the conservation of all our natural resources, are essentially democratic in spirit, purpose, and method. **1916**

Henry Beetle Hough

Now we know there are degrees even in death. All around us nature is full of casualties, but they do not interrupt the stream of life. When most living things die, they seem only to revert to the central theme of existence from which they were temporarily detached. There is a spirit of vitality everywhere which enfolds the dead with a countenance of consolation, and bestows upon the living races more than has been taken away. But to the heath hen something more than death has happened, or, rather, a different kind of death. There is no survivor, there is no future, there is no life to be recreated in this form again. We are looking upon the uttermost finality which can be written, glimpsing the darkness which will not know another ray of light. We are in touch with the reality of extinction.

It is written that the heath hen had ceased long ago to be of economic importance, and that it could never have been of economic importance again. It follows, therefore, that preservation of this bird was a matter of sentiment alone, since between economic usefulness and sentiment our world knows no middle ground. The heath hen was a curious creature, an actor out of place, surviving beyond its appointed days, simply because there happened to be a bit of scenery fortuitously at hand for the playing of a last dramatic act and a sentimental epilogue. The bird we are speaking of was the

prairie chicken of the east, and the contradiction in terms is clear, for where in the east is there a prairie, or any suitable environment for a bird not of the forest nor of the sea nor of the air, but of the open range? By chance there is a great plain on Martha's Vineyard, and despite the fact that the island is relatively small, it has never been considered amiss to speak of the vastness of this great plain of scrub oak, sweet fern, alder, blasted pine—and of the heath hen. Here, then, in sound of the roaring surf, the prairie chicken of the east died, a single specimen making an end of the race, somewhere alone in the brush.

The heath hen failed to adapt to changing conditions and fell a victim to the laws of natural selection. This is a curious thing, for until the white men took over the land, the heath hen had achieved an admirable adaptation, embodying such fine distinctions of nature that scientists appreciate their nicety and would like to understand them better. Even if you knew where a heath hen was, against a background of twigs and brush, you could not see it unless it moved. Failed to adapt! Why, no creature was ever more at home, more nicely adjusted to place and time than the heath hen on the Vineyard plains! The whole trouble lay in the fact that the heath hen was a bird man could kill, and so it had to die. A wild bird in a thicket and a man in a house cannot be neighbors, for cats will be turned loose and forced to forage, fire will burn over the landscape time and time again, and there are even diseases of the domestic poultry yard to menace wild things.

In recent years an impression has gone forth that man has learned to withhold his hand and to let things about him grow and multiply. The gospel of conservation, it is said, has won the day. We know this is not true. May the death of the heath hen serve to bring us nearer a time of realization and fulfillment! Until now, saving only the imperious grace of economic importance and sometimes not even that, a creature that man could kill has had to die.

1933

MARTHA'S VINEYARD, HOME OF THE LAST HEATH HENS

The Last Parakeet

"CAROLINA PARAQUETS" BY JOHN A. RUTHVEN, 1968

While Martha, the famous last passenger pigeon, waited out her days in the zoo at Cincinnati, she had neighbors who were likewise doomed to extinction. Martha went down to lasting fame, the hour of her death faithfully recorded. Incredibly, in a nearby cage, the last known of the brilliant little green-and-yellow Carolina parakeets died and disappeared like a wisp of smoke, so ignored by the world that the details surrounding its passing became a mystery.

One day recently [1968], Cincinnati bird artist John Ruthven and I decided to see what we could learn about the last parakeets. As we tracked the vanished bird it seemed unreal that the parakeets had once flown in colorful flocks along the nearby Ohio River. They were bright green with lemon-yellow heads and necks, and a splash of brilliant orange on their foreheads. Including the length of their tails, which was considerable, they were twelve to thirteen inches long. Their legs were short. Their hooked bills possessed great strength for their size. The lower mandible had sharp edges which apparently served the birds well in cutting open tough-shelled seeds of such plants as the cocklebur.

Audubon observed that when a flock of parakeets came to a feeding area they did not alight at once. Instead they would circle at considerable height, "gradually lowering until they almost touch the ground, when suddenly re-ascending they all settle on the tree that bears the fruit of which they are in quest."

The Carolina parakeet was apparently a spunky bird. Instead of lapsing into a possumlike trance or trauma, he would reach for the human hand that tried to hold him. And if he succeeded in getting a grip he left a serious cut to mark the spot.

Parakeets made good pets, however, were easily domesticated, and consequently were often collected in large numbers for the cage-bird trade.

Early ornithologists noted that the parakeets had a strong preference for the seeds of the cocklebur. This native weed grew in abundance in river bottoms and thrived in newly cleared fields.

Once having found a field of cockleburs, the parakeets would flock back to it at the feeding hour day after day until the supply was exhausted. From their roosting or nesting areas, usually deep in the heart of a swamp forest, they would come hurtling along, moving in a straight line as long as no obstacle appeared in their paths.

If the Carolina parakeet had been content to subsist on cockleburs it might not have suffered extinction quite as early as it did. But the parakeet was an opportunist. Once settlers had their orchards established, the adaptable parakeets were quick to note the change. Where they had previously crawled over the stems of cockleburs and other wild seed-bearing plants, they now decorated apple and pear trees. They also settled so thickly on shocks of harvested grain they reminded Audubon of a green carpet thrown over the stack.

In the fruit trees, they were said to have moved along the limbs — even before the fruit had ripened — and take one fruit at a time, crush it open for the seeds, then drop it on the ground, until the tree was stripped.

Hard-pressed farmers, as one might expect, took a dim view of such robbery. It was simple enough for the offended farmer to approach within range of the marauding parakeets and commit "great slaughter among them."

What would the parakeets do as a wounded member of their flock fell to the ground? They would wheel and turn and come back, screeching all the while and flying above their fallen companion until they too were within gun range. In this manner whole flocks could sometimes be decimated.

The bird was considered by many to be choice table fare, and parakeets that invited themselves to dine in the farmer's orchard often ended up at dinner in his house. They were also collected to provide colorful hat decorations for ladies with a preference for green feathers.

What part each of these elements played in the bird's disappearance will never be fully known. Changes in habitat may well have accounted for the greatest losses.

Whatever the cause, Carolina parakeet populations fell with startling speed. In a brief 25 years during the early part of the 1800s, Audubon noted that parakeets had gone from plentiful to scarce. Once they had occupied a range covering the Southeastern section of the country, west to central Texas, north to Colorado and southern Wisconsin, and eastward to the District of Columbia. Throughout their wide range, if they were spotted after 1870, it was rarely, and then usually in small flocks. Seldom were they pests in orchard and field any longer. In a few lonely and remote swamp forests in Florida they were still encountered into the 1890s. Bird collectors by this time were eagerly seeking out parakeets, catching them alive when possible, and selling them to zoological gardens.

Sometime during this period — the date is not recorded — the Cincinnati Zoo bought sixteen parakeets out of Florida, at $2.50 each. Among them was the bird that would become the final member of his species.

George Laycock

Men, Birds, and Adventure

An added refinement and a new zest were added to birding when men went out with microphones to capture bird songs on records. It became the absorbing aim of Albert R. Brand and Arthur A. Allen of Cornell University to record the voices of all American birds while they were still with us, particularly those which were in danger of becoming extinct. This pioneering expedition, like none ever known before, was sponsored by the American Museum of Natural History and Cornell University.

With motion picture cameras, a sound truck, and large parabolic reflectors to funnel sound into the microphones as birds moved about, the expedition took off in 1935 on a trip of fifteen thousand miles. Paul Kellogg of Cornell was sound technician and George Sutton was artist. James Tanner, a graduate student in ornithology, was assistant in photography and sound recording, and a general handy man who provided unquenchable amounts of enthusiasm when it began to flag in the older members of the party. Mr. Brand and Dr. Allen controlled the route and procedure of this unique expedition.

The first project was to record the voices of the nearly extinct ivory-billed woodpeckers. Dr. Allen had seen them in 1924 in certain remote swamps in central Florida. There was no way of knowing whether the big woodpeckers were still in existence. A species so near extinction could have died out in that time. In Florida the sound truck went into the swamps which were sus-

pected of concealing the rare birds; when it bogged down the men walked and waded. But they had no luck. No ivory-bills could be located. The ornithologists realized that they might even now be too late to record the voices of these birds.

In late March of 1935 the crew started for Louisiana where, in deep swamp forests along the Tensas River, someone in 1932 had reported having seen ivory-bills. This was in northern Louisiana, almost due west of Vicksburg, Mississippi. The truck went as far as it could until deep water barred the way. The road, what there was of it, lay submerged in a spring flood. Yet the region was too alluring and too promising to give up now. Here was an unbroken forest stretching eighteen miles in one direction and thirty miles in another. Somewhere in there, among the buttressed cypresses and big tupelos and gums, in a swamp spilling over with spring song, ivory-billed woodpeckers might possibly be nesting.

There is more than one way to navigate high water. The men left the sound equipment and truck in a comparatively dry place and then went in on foot to explore. They borrowed a pirogue from a Cajun and paddled among the cypresses—listening, looking, wondering.

It was like a jungle, a wet world filled with singing prothonotary warblers, the buzzing calls of parula warblers, the explosive comments of the white-eyed vireos, the loud caroling of Carolina wrens and the staccato hammering of woodpeckers—but not the sounds that were so keenly sought. Spring migration was in full swing and the treetops were alive with northbound, singing birds. Down at the level of the swamp, water snakes, some of them cottonmouth moccasins, sunning themselves, were draped on bare branches and dead wood over the brown water. Turtles, sometimes piled up three deep, made their retreat when the questing pirogue approached too close. Now and then an alligator submerged in the dark water.

Seven miles from the road, and after three days of exploring, they found the ivory-billed woodpeckers. Incredible, rare, magnificent, prehistoric-looking— there they were, nesting in a cypress. It was an historic moment which very easily might never be repeated. In the days of Catesby, Audubon, Wilson, and Du Pratz, the ivory-bills were noticeable and to be commented

---

Ivory-billed woodpeckers were fairly common in southern America when Mark Catesby published this illustration in 1731. But two centuries later, ornithologists slogging through the swamps of northern Louisiana (above) would discover only five in three years of searching.

upon, but they were not considered particularly rare. Yet, it is probable that they were never as abundant as the red-headed woodpecker or even the big pileated, which comes closer to the magnificence and size of the ivory-bill, but which does not have the peculiar demands for subsistence of the latter.

The ivory-billed woodpecker is twenty inches long. The male has a brilliant scarlet crest standing straight back in line with the ivory-white beak, which is like a great blunt chisel. A long white stripe down the side of the black head, neck, and back joins the white patches on the wings. The breast, tail, and the rest of the wing-surface are glossy black. The ivory-bill is unique. We will never see his like again.

Each pair of ivory-bills needs about six square miles of primeval forest in which to subsist. In a similar space, Dr. Allen estimated that perhaps 126 pairs of red-bellied woodpeckers might find home and food and room to fly, or thirty-six pairs of the big pileated woodpeckers. The ivory-bill evidently requires as a food source those trees which have been dead for only two or three years. When the first insects get into the outer wood and their borers chew tunnels under the bark, the tree is ready for the ivory-billed woodpecker. With a wooden sound of wings and a *clunk!* the bird claps against the resonant side of the dead trunk. Then there is a heavy thumping, like an ax on a log, and great slabs of bark are torn away and flung to the ground as the bird goes after the fat white grubs that lie beneath. When the woodpecker is finished with a tree, it moves on to another, leaving the barked tree for the red-heads to hammer, the red-bellies to pound, the pileateds to chop. Into abandoned holes may come chickadees and prothonotary warblers to nest. Flying squirrels or screech owls may take over the cavity.

Since the ivory-billed woodpecker requires the peculiar situation of newly-dead trees in a primeval forest, an area of some size can, therefore, support only a few. There simply are not enough or ever were enough of its special grubs to feed more than a limited population of ivory-bills.

No one knew these facts until Dr. Allen's expedition with the sound equipment went into the Louisiana swamps. The young graduate student from Cornell, James Tanner, returned later to pursue the study. He had become imbued with that feeling of conquest, that search for adventure and the spirit of dedication of a man pioneering in science. He determined to learn all there was to know about the ivory-billed woodpeckers before they became extinct. James Tanner devoted three years of his life to the project. He traveled more than forty-five thousand miles—on foot, by car, on horseback, by boat—into nearly all the southern forests where ivory-bills either had been reported or in which he suspected they might still live.

But back to Dr. Allen's expedition in 1935, with the sound truck still at the edge of the swamp, seven miles from the nest of the ivory-billed woodpeckers. A sound truck with 1,800 pounds of equipment does not easily navigate a swampy terrain which has recently had an additional supply of water from the spring rise.

They drove back, therefore, to the nearest town and obtained the cooperation of the mayor and the sheriff. The truck was dismantled, and everything in it was set up in the bed of an old, unpainted, solid, and serviceable farm wagon. After the precious contents were bolted firmly in place, the wagon was hitched to four mules. The animals plodded down the dirt road to the edge of the swamp; they kept on going. While the wagon groaned and rocked and sucked at the muddy depths, and while the owners of all that expensive and highly cherished equipment no doubt held their collective breaths, the wagon finally reached the spot where there was comparatively solid ground, only three hundred feet from the nest of what might possibly be the last pair of ivory-billed woodpeckers in the world.

The men set up camp. To make a dry base, they cut piles of palmetto fans and made a thatch flooring at the

base of a huge water oak. A 24-power binocular on a tripod, like a telescope, was set up and a camp chair was placed before the eye piece. The lens was focused on the nest hole so that attention could be paid to whatever was going on up there, while the microphone with its "sound mirror" faithfully recorded the calls, the talking, the guttural sounds that came from the cavity.

The men were there for eight days. When the woodpeckers became accustomed to human presence, a blind was built in a neighboring tree; it was set up level with the nest and not more than twenty feet away from the opening through which the adult birds flew several times a day.

The whole experience was something which none of the four would ever forget. They made the recording for posterity. Then they went back to town, reassembled the sound truck, and set off for Oklahoma to record the booming of the lesser prairie chickens on a spring dawn, and for Colorado to photograph and record the golden eagles and many other western birds.

By the time the summer's adventure was over, they had exposed almost ten miles of film and had recorded the voices of more than one hundred species of American birds. But it was the ivory-billed woodpeckers, perhaps more than any other birds studied and recorded, which held the greatest thrill and meaning to the men who started the expedition.

Virginia S. Eifert

Take a Long, Last Look at the Condor

The sun has been up for an hour now, and currents of warm air have begun to rise from the California canyon floors. Hopping awkwardly along a high ledge, a huge black bird with a naked gray neck and a reddish-orange head flaps its wings a few times, rides the thermal draft upward in enormous spirals and glides away to the south. You stand and watch, awed, and then look around, half expecting to see a saber-toothed cat, a woolly mammoth, a giant dire wolf or a big short-faced bear. For that soaring creature is *Gymnogyps Californianus*, the California condor, largest land bird in North America and perhaps the last remnant of the distant past that saw man's own beginnings.

Although it trails a million years or more behind it, the California condor, as a species, may be very near its end. In the past century, condors have almost vanished from the face of the earth, casualties of man's conquest of the continent.

The California condors were well established in North America when the first men arrived over the land bridge from Siberia to Alaska. They were common all the way down the Pacific coast into Mexico and across the whole southern half of the present United States. Inevitably, west coast Indians created legends about them. The Tlingit people, for instance, said the condor made the thunder by flapping its wings and shot lightning from its eyes. Similar legends grew up among other tribes, and the condor became the coastal Indians' thunderbird. It was feared and worshiped, and it became a familiar figure on the totem poles, as well as in ornamentation.

By the 1850s, however, the condor population was waning. The early Spanish settlers in California did little to disturb the birds. In fact, their dead cattle provided more than ample food for the condors. Then came the Mexican War, discovery of nuggets at Sutter's millrace and the gold rush. Partly out of bravado, the gold-miners began to shoot condors—such big birds *had* to be dangerous.

While the condors were thus being killed by miners, collectors were at work "saving nature." Museums and private collectors assembled displays of birds' eggs and, because they were so scarce, condor eggs became extremely valuable. The only condors then surviving were in the rugged mountains east of Santa Barbara, but the collectors found them.

Not until the 1920s was there any great interest in the condor's plight. In 1926, the famed explorer and ornithologist William Beebe declared: "The condor's doom is near. Within a few years at most the last individual will have perished." Since then a number of surveys have been undertaken and the most recent data indicate that the total condor population remains somewhere between 40 and 60 [Between 30 and 40 now. Ed.].

Normally, only one egg is laid each year by a female condor and it takes six weeks to hatch. If that egg is broken or stolen early, the bird may lay another to replace it, but not if the brooding time is half gone. Once hatched, the chick is dependent for at least seven months, often as long as a year. With a dependent chick, the mother condor doesn't lay an egg that spring but waits another year. That averages out to one egg every other year, and the young birds do not mate until they are six or seven years old. At that production rate, it doesn't take many accidents to wipe out a whole population.

Today, man remains the condor's principal enemy. Although it is illegal to shoot the birds, a few are shot from time to time by ignorant or irresponsible gunners. Poisoned carcasses used by ranchers to kill coyotes are also a constant hazard to the condor, which is a scavenger.

In 1937, a small roosting and nesting area was set aside for condors in Sisquoc canyon in California's Los Padres National Forest. In 1951, a much larger area (53,000 acres) was designated as the Sespe Condor Sanctuary 50 miles farther south in Ventura County. But in both places problems are created by man.

Condors are easily disturbed, often becoming moody and confused. They are cat-curious and will watch a man in their area for hours. (One was seen to perch in the same tree 22 hours, watching a condor-watcher.) If people come too near, however, or stay too long—or if loud noises persist even a mile away—the condors simply move out, deserting nest, egg or chick if necessary.

Thus far, the condors have been saved from extinction by the work of half a dozen organizations and perhaps a hundred determined individuals, backed by thousands of others. Unless the campaign is substantially broadened, though, the species' days are numbered.

Why even try to save "those forty dirty birds," as some call them? As scavengers, condors have a vitally important role to play in nature's scheme of things. Beyond that, however, the condor must be saved simply because it is a part of the great, infinitely varied stream of life. And since it is one of the last living links with man's own beginnings, the condor may well have something to tell us—if we would only pause and listen—about time . . . and change . . . and enduring.

Hal Borland

The View from Hawk Mountain

The first hawk of the day appears, soundlessly, rising out of the trees below us this fine, mid-September morning. The time is not yet nine o'clock daylight-saving time—eight o'clock *bird time*, as we say, or standard time. The day is warm, the fog is burning out of the valleys, and the air has begun to rise, stirring the hawk's impulse to get moving south. It flaps once or twice, then stretches its rounded wings flat into a plane about three feet from tip to tip, and turns slowly in a small circle, feeling for the buoyant air that will lift it. The bird's back and wings are brown, with a touch of olive; the short tail is barred with wide black and white stripes.

"*There's* a broadwing," says one of my companions on North Lookout. This is a weekday, but already there are six of us sitting here on favored boulders, facing east along the spine of the Kittatinny ridge.

"He isn't getting much lift yet."

As it circles below us, the broad-winged hawk manages the air with slight adjustments of its tail and wing feathers. It spreads the tail and the primaries—the first 10 feathers at the back edge of each wing, from the wing tip in; spreads them wide to catch the air, closes a few, twists them for control as it turns, draws all together as it sideslips, spreads the feathers again, circles, flaps once, twice, three times for more altitude, circles—not yet at eye level, feathers twisting, flaring, narrowing, flicking. It is unbelievable that any creature should have such delicate control over so many of its parts.

"Well, buddy, where are your brethren?"—addressed to the hawk.

"It's early yet."

"Oh-oh, there they are: one, two, three, four—see, Charlie, under the Hunters' Field."

"Right. I've got another bunch over here, to the left of that."

Someone else finds a third group, then a fourth. Broadwings that set down on the ridge at the end of yesterday's flight are now getting up from perches all over the slopes below us, circling for altitude, seeking the updrafts, ganging up into the groups in which they will travel. This will be a good day at Hawk Mountain.

The Kittatinny ridge rises in New York State and, virtually unbroken, marches across northern New Jersey and eastern Pennsylvania all the way to the Maryland border. The Indians gave the ridge its name; Kittatinny means "endless mountain." There are some short outrider ridges between this ridge and the distant sea, but the Kittatinny is essentially the southeast edge of the Appalachian chain.

When the hawks leave their breeding territories in eastern Canada and the northeastern states and move toward the south in the fall—some to winter in New England, some to stop in the Middle Atlantic states, some to go on, even as far as South America—many of them make for the Atlantic coastline and follow that. But large numbers, particularly of the hawks that like to soar, stay inland and follow the Appalachians. The heat rising and the wind rebounding off the mountains provides lift—sheets of rising air—on which they can ride and so cover long distances with relatively little effort.

If the weather is right and the lift is good, they cling to a ridge even when it bends due west. If there's a long break in the ridge or an interrupting jumble of cross-ridges, the hawks look to the south for something better, tack that way to the new air, and ride those currents until something farther south attracts them away. So, striking the Appalachians to the west and north and east, they drop south, ridge to ridge. Sometimes the weather conditions and the topography combine to create a flow directly southward, across the grain of the mountains, and they drift with it, without tacking. The Kittatinny is the last of the great ridges they reach. Beyond it is the Great Valley, the beginning of the lowlands that end at the sea. When the hawks reach the endless mountain, a good many of them stay with it. On some days they pile up by the thousands.

Not quite halfway along its course through eastern Pennsylvania—where it is called Blue Mountain for its entire length—the Kittatinny bends west, then southwest, then west again; begins to dip gradually, narrows into a hogback that grows progressively sharper for two miles. Suddenly it rises steeply to a field of sandstone boulders, a field that from the air has the shape of an arrowhead. Just there, the ridge twists abruptly, almost doubling back on itself, and after several miles of zigzagging toward the southeast finally does send out a long spur back toward the northeast as it turns and resumes its southwesterly course. On the inside of the ragged bowl thus created, the flanks of the ridge and its headlands are steep; in places, sandstone cliffs jut out through the trees. The bowl and the stone outcroppings form an amphitheater that looks out on a spectacular migration.

The boulder field shaped like an arrowhead points southwest. In the old days, there was irony in that topographic whimsy: every fall, thousands of migrating birds of prey got no farther southwest than the pointing arrow. Gunners posted themselves there and on the other stone outcroppings and shot at the passing birds. Broadwings and redtails and red-shoulders and roughlegs and golden eagles and bald eagles and sharpshins and Cooper's hawks and goshawks and peregrines and merlins and kestrels and harriers and ospreys fell dead, or maimed—in the end, the same—into the tops of the red and golden trees.

It is forty years since that last happened here, on what has come to be called Hawk Mountain. Hawkwatchers now roost in the arrow-shaped field of boulders—the North Lookout of Hawk Mountain Sanctuary—and on the other outcroppings, all looking to the east, into the line of flight.

So here I am, once again nestled down on a soft rock, as they say here, with the boulder field dipping gradually down in front of me. There's a big-toothed aspen near the center of the lookout, a tree kept small by the weather; off to one side is a clump of mountain laurel and rhododendron and a mountain ash that bears bright red berries in the fall. All around the front and sides of the lookout are the tops of hemlocks, their roots on the slopes below, and at the back, birches, oaks, black gums, maples, mountain holly, witch hazel, and shoots of American chestnut.

This is my first visit here of the fall hawk-migration season. Between now and the end of November, I will make two or three such visits, as I do each fall I can, driving west from my home in Connecticut. It is a long way to go to look at birds—a half-day's drive each way. But others regularly come from farther away—Ohio, Georgia, Canada. And, anyway, to me Hawk Mountain is much more than a place to look at birds. More than that, the feeling these passing birds give me—that I am somehow at the very heart of the migration—is something I have never experienced anywhere else. Most migration seems to take place almost by magic. You don't see it happening, partly because so much of it goes on at night; suddenly one morning the front lawn is swarming with robins or white-throated sparrows. But at Hawk Mountain the flow of southing birds is visible; it goes on and on during a good day, giving an inkling of the breadth and depth of the movement.

My trips to the mountain have become an annual ritual. My explorations after birds at Hawk Mountain and elsewhere have led me into the much larger arena of the world's environment. One cannot spend much time looking for wildlife in the urban Northeast without becoming sensitized to the pressures man is putting on the space in which he lives. I began writing about it. My attitude toward birding changed; I narrowed my focus and spent less and less time trying to add new birds to my Life List. To be sure, I still like to find new birds. But it is clear to me that there are great gaps in man's knowledge about birds, as there are great gaps in his knowledge of the working of all nature and his place in it. That problem attracts me.

Hawk Mountain is engaged, in part, in filling a few of those gaps. For forty years, it has been the only place in the Northeast where the migration of the birds of prey has been observed on a daily basis throughout the fall. Almost since the beginning of the sanctuary's existence, counts of the passing hawks have been made, to develop a picture of the mechanics and timing of the migration, and to give some very rough clues to the numbers and make-up of the northeastern hawk population. The effort is one the experienced amateur can participate in. In fact, because the paid staff of Hawk Mountain Sanctuary is so small, it has to depend on

Nearly half a century ago, hawks were considered vermin and enemies to birds and other game. Massive kills like the one above, photographed in 1932, were often recorded during fall migration at Hawk Mountain in Pennsylvania. Such spectacles prompted conservationists to purchase the mountain and turn it into Hawk Mountain Sanctuary. Thus ended the mountain's 60 to 70 year history as the "graveyard of hawks" and began its history as a center for studies of raptors.

those amateurs to do a great deal of the counting. So when I come to Hawk Mountain in the fall, I come to help with the count and, generally, to take an active role in a valuable environmental venture, as well as to place myself in the dramatic landscape, and in the middle of the passage of the birds of prey.

Down to the right of North Lookout, along the first southeastward bend of the Hawk Mountain zigzag, are four outcroppings of stone. The farthest away, about half a mile off, is South Lookout. Both North and South will be manned today, sharing the job of counting. The two lookouts are connected by walkie-talkies, so as to prevent double counting and to allow us to keep each other apprised of approaching birds.

I have put a pillow between me and the sandstone boulders of the lookouts. Twice in the past I've gone through a pair of pants on these rocks, from not bringing some sort of cushion, or not using it once I'd brought it. The regulars carry their pillows under their arms or in knapsacks with their lunches, pillows of great variety — slabs of foam rubber, air chairs, ancient army blankets, ponchos, throw pillows carefully recovered with sturdy canvas and sometimes embroidered with the owner's name. A few old-timers arrive on North Lookout wearing their pillows like reverse aprons tied around the waist, so that when they move from rock to rock their pillows stay with them. Necessity is the mother of invention.

The prospect from this mountaintop is tremendous. Views 20 or 30 miles long stretch out to an arc of horizon 70 miles around. I used not to appreciate it much. I have never been comfortable with heights, and when, on my first visit to the sanctuary, having trudged up the two-thirds of a mile through the woods until I was out in the open, I found myself on the brink of a ledge, looking out across the broad valley to the north, with the world a quarter of a mile almost straight down, I felt as if I had lost the better part of my specific gravity. And every autumn since, when I have made my first climb to North Lookout, I have felt echoing twinges. But, despite that, I now walk down onto the lookout and take in the view and feel I have come home.

Wherever I am, when the wind is in the northwest and the air has a bite to it, the view from Hawk Mountain spreads itself before me in my memory and I long to be a part of it — the ancient upthrust mountains, the enormous space, the rhythms of weather, the passing of birds that are the essence of wildness, all speaking of measures of time that dwarf man.

Michael Harwood

Egrets and the Plume Trade

Feathers were the crowning glory for ladies' hats in the early years of the twentieth century—and that didn't mean just a feather or two. Whole birds were sometimes mounted precariously atop the crown of a hat.

London, Paris, and New York were the centers of the millinery trade in those days, and bird skins by the millions flowed through these cities: the skins of herons and egrets, parrots and hummingbirds, birds of paradise, and many others. In just one season, that of 1892, a single "feather merchant" of Jacksonville, Florida, shipped 130,000 bird skins to New York for the trade. In that same year, many other similar shipments were being assembled in other parts of North America, and in South America, Africa, Asia, Australia, and New Guinea as well. The plume trade was vast, well-organized, and well-financed.

In North America the principal victims were the snowy egret and the common egret—beautiful herons that had at one time been familiar birds with a widespread distribution. The two species bred in colonies, with hundreds of nests often built close beside each other in low-branched trees in Southern swamps. During the breeding season the adults developed special courtship plumes called aigrettes, which were especially prized. Descending on a nesting colony, plume hunters could utterly destroy it in a day or two. They killed all the adult birds for their feathers, then left the eggs and young birds to die.

By the turn of the century, egrets had disappeared nearly everywhere in Florida, their former stronghold in the United States. In other Southern states the story was about the same—with one notable exception, Louisiana. Here a sizeable flock of egrets still nested at the Avery Island Preserve, a private sanctuary established by E. A. McIlhenny, an enthusiastic and affluent conservationist. He and a few other ardent champions of embattled wildlife were fighting to preserve the plume birds.

The various Audubon clubs that had sprung up around the country since 1885 were among the organizations that led the battle. They secured their first notable success in 1901 with the passage of a Florida law protecting nongame birds—including all of the species especially valued for their plumes. The next year the clubs consolidated their position by banding together into a National Association of Audubon Societies, with William Dutcher, a militant conservationist, as the first president.

The Audubon clubs came to the fore just in time, for in 1903 only eighteen specimens of the common egret

could be discovered in the entire state of Florida—those in the Cuthbert rookery in the Everglades.

The fledgling National Audubon Society promptly employed four wardens to patrol and protect the remaining rookeries of water birds in the state. Young Guy Bradley was one of the four; his territory was Monroe County, which covered Florida's Lower Keys.

On July 8, 1905, Bradley heard shots coming from the direction of the Oyster Keys, near his home. Getting into his boat, he set out to investigate—and was never seen alive again, except by the poachers who killed him. The murderers were never punished for their act, for lack of concrete legal evidence against them. But they were known, and some of their cronies learned what had happened. As Bradley had approached the poachers' anchored schooner, two of the plume hunters had also been returning to it in a small boat loaded with dead birds. Bradley attempted to arrest the men and was shot by a third poacher, who was standing on the deck of the schooner. The raiders promptly sailed away from the area, and some hours later Bradley's body, a bullet hole in the neck, was found in his drifting boat.

A wave of indignation swept the country over the murder, and the feeling against plume hunters became even more pronounced in 1908 when a second Audubon warden was shot and killed as he attempted to protect a rookery in South Carolina. Because of the widespread resentment over such acts and the publicity campaign launched by the National Association of Audubon Societies, an Audubon Plumage Bill was pushed through the New York State Legislature in 1910. This act banned the sale of wild-bird plumage anywhere in the state, including New York City, the center of America's millinery trade. In 1913 the federal government reinforced this law with an act barring the importation of wild-bird plumage of any sort into the United States. After that, state after state followed the lead of New York and prohibited commerce in plumage—and the fight was won.

After their near brush with extermination in the United States, the recovery of the snowy and American egrets has been miraculous. Now they are common throughout the South and much of the East during the breeding season, and during their post-breeding flights they can be seen widely throughout much of the rest of the country.

— **Robert McClung**

The glamorous filigree of the snowy egret's nuptial plumes, or aigrettes (left), made egrets the target of hunters supplying the millinery trade in the late 1800's, when aigrette-adorned hats (above) were fashionable.

Adventures in Bird Protection

The year 1908 was a banner one in bird protection, for it saw the birth of two new wildlife reservations—Malheur in Oregon and Lower Klamath in southern Oregon and northern California—dedicated to the protection of migratory ducks and geese. Previous reservations had been created for non-edible water birds. The two were similar in appearance and their fates have paralleled each other strangely. This is part of Malheur's story.

Malheur was appropriately, even prophetically, named. It lies in the arid sage brush country of Harney County, Oregon. Ornithologically it was discovered by Captain Charles E. Bendire in the early 1870's, but its wonders were brought to public attention by William L. Finley who, with Herman T. Bohlman, in the year 1908 spent five weeks photographing in its marshy vastness. Finley's report to the Audubon Association was the means of its being declared a Federal bird reserve on August 18th of that year.

One day in 1916, with the game-warden, I witnessed its amazing spectacles of bird life. Among the feathered hosts were avocets, grebes, killdeers, phalaropes, stilts and willets. There were three kinds of terns, also redheads, ruddys, cinnamon teal and other ducks. As our little boat proceeded, white pelicans, glossy ibises, cormorants, gulls and great blue herons came into view. There were thousands of Canada geese. Wings everywhere in the tules, on the shores, among the interminable jumble of islands, on the water and in the sky. It would have been an easy matter to shoot a boat-load of birds. But such things were not being done here. Now it was a vast bird nursery, more than one hundred and forty square miles in extent and no one with a gun was permitted to enter its precincts.

A disquieting story reached me. The Governor of Oregon and members of the State Land Board had left the region just before my arrival. It was said they claimed that the land belonged to the State and steps were to be taken to clear up this title and drain the lake for farm lands. The lake bottom, when once the water had been removed, would make a magnificent farming community.

This was the beginning of a fight for the possession of Malheur Lake which was to continue for nineteen years before a settlement could be reached. On one side were the Biological Survey, the Oregon Audubon Society and the National Association of Audubon Societies trying to save the lake for the birds; the opposition came from the State of Oregon through its engineering department, abetted at every turn by commercially minded persons who wanted the region drained for farm lands.

Finley was the active director in many of the hardfought battles that ensued. He led an effort in the Oregon Legislature to pass a bill to cede to the United States Government any rights that Oregon might have to the lake. The bill was defeated. He was also the moving spirit in an Initiative to declare Malheur Lake the "Roosevelt Bird Refuge."

The contest over the Initiative was a bitter one. The issue at stake on November 2, 1920, was that if the people of the State voted our way the birds could keep their old home; but if we lost, the lake was to be destroyed and its dried bed sold for the benefit of the State School Fund.

Just before the vote, the would-be land developers widely distributed a card showing a picture of a little girl and a white pelican, which bore the legend, VOTE FOR THE BABY. From all the feathered inhabitants of Malheur, our opponents cleverly chose the pelican on account of the popular prejudice against it as a fish-eating bird. An avalanche of adverse ballots lost us the Initiative.

The Solicitor of the U.S. Department of Agriculture decided that the Federal Government had some rights to the water of the Silvies and Blitzen rivers, without which the lake would soon evaporate. By 1921, therefore, plans were completed for filing an injunction restraining the State from making too free use of the water.

But the injunction was never filed. Just at the most effective moment an Oregon Congressman descended on the Biological Survey for a parley. This resulted in calling a conference at Salem, Oregon. Here a representative of the Survey, like Solomon of old, proposed to divide the disputed property, except that in this case

---

The strident message of the political placard (above left) opposing creation of the Malheur refuge ignored not only the need for a protected home for wildlife but also the appeal of observing such inhabitants as the black-crowned night herons silhouetted at right.

a dyke instead of a sword was to be used. But Oregon would not agree to partition the lake into two parts by a dyke; what it wanted was all the water for its citizens.

The Eastern Oregon Live Stock Company secured large holdings south of Malheur, and in time diverted the waters of the Blitzen on to the desert to make hay lands for stock. Ranchers to the north of the lake likewise used the flow of the Silvies and before many years Malheur Lake, robbed of its sources of water, became a barren waste. No wild life was left. The earth was baked and cracked and burnt; and in the alkali dust curled the whitened forms of fish, and the horns and heads of long-dead bison came to view. Malheur, the Wonderful, had become Gehenna, the Place of Death.

WILSON'S PHALAROPE

SANDHILL CRANES AND CANADA GEESE

Years went by, during which a few ranchers grazed cattle or raised meager crops on the edge of what formerly was the lake-bed. Every spring and autumn ducks and geese came over, circled about for a time and, finding no place to alight, continued on over the uplands of gray and purple sage. Now and then a wandering gull flew by with a discordant cry. The greatest area for water-birds in all our vast Western country was no more. The friends of the birds were too few and their arms were too weak to withstand the combined attacks of politics and commercialism.

Thus time passed, until 1934, when unbelievably good fortune befell. Mr. Jay N. Darling, the new Chief of the Bureau of Biological Survey, secured $675,000 from the Public Works Administration, bought the Eastern Oregon Live Stock Company's holdings of 64,717 acres, and cut the dam which lay on the Blitzen. Waters again began flowing into the parched basin of Malheur. That fall, in migration time, the 4,000 acres of water that already had accumulated were covered with happy ducks, and the settlers around Malheur's perimeters were rapidly departing. Malheur was saved.

—————————————**Thomas Gilbert Pearson**

By 1934, when the dam holding back water from Malheur Lake was cut, the area had become a dry, desolate wasteland (above). Today, the majesty of Malheur is reflected in the 227 species of birds (including those at right) regularly found in its 180,850 acres of freshwater marshes, meadows, and shallow lakes.

HORNED GREBES

YELLOW-HEADED BLACKBIRD

DOUBLE-CRESTED CORMORANTS

Triumph of the Trumpeters

In the lonely wilderness of southwestern Montana lies the wild and spacious Centennial Valley. Surrounded by snow-capped mountains rising to 10,000 feet, the valley itself nestles at 6,600 feet above sea level and contains great marshes, three shallow blue lakes, and several sparkling streams inhabited by big rainbow, brook and cutthroat trout and some of the last native grayling in the contiguous United States. It is a beautiful and untroubled spot.

It is here that one of the rarest and most beautiful of waterfowl, the wild trumpeter swan, lives and multiplies in Red Rock Lakes National Wildlife Refuge. Once near extinction, with only 73 birds left in the United States, the trumpeter made its last stand in Centennial Valley, where waters warmed by thermal springs spared it the hazards of migration. Protected there since 1935, they have now increased to a flock of several hundred, and their stock has been reintroduced to Oregon, Nevada, Wyoming and South Dakota.

There was a time when the trumpeter ranged over much of the central part of the continent—from Alaska to Iowa, Missouri and Indiana—and wintered in vast numbers in the Ohio and Mississippi valleys, along the Gulf of Mexico, and in the lower Columbia River. Occasionally it was seen even on the Atlantic Coast.

In earlier years, the Indians and Eskimos caught and killed some of the birds, and natural enemies such as eagles and coyotes sometimes made off with the baby swans or cygnets, but the trumpeter was able to withstand these drains. It was the white man who brought this handsome creature almost to extinction. Tender young swans were relished by the pioneer settlers as a pleasant change from a steady diet of deer and buffalo, and the fur trade soon learned that swan skins and quills were a lucrative commodity in the market place. Trumpeter down made the best powder puffs, quilts and featherbeds, and the quills, which are very hard but elastic, were perfect for pens.

Market hunters and settlers killed thousands of trumpeters and whistlers in all seasons of the year. The

Hudson's Bay Company alone sold 17,671 swan skins in London between 1853 and 1877, and it is probable that most of these were from trumpeters. There are no figures on the vast numbers sold in this country and abroad by other companies and individuals.

Moreover, around the turn of the century, a great demand developed for these spectacular birds for zoos, private collections, parks and estates. The young were run down and captured in September before they could fly; they brought $50 a pair, a comfortable sum in those days, and were shipped all over the United States and across the Atlantic. Residents of Montana's Red Rock Lakes country developed such a thriving business in baby swans that they managed to talk the market hunters into sparing some breeding pairs. It is quite possible that this is partially responsible for the fact that the trumpeters survived at all.

In 1900 market hunting was outlawed by Federal statute, and the adoption of the Migratory Bird Treaty Act with Great Britain in 1918 ended all hunting of swans.

But these measures came almost too late to save the trumpeters. In 1912 the famous ornithologist, Edward Howe Forbush, wrote sadly: "The Trumpeter has succumbed to incessant persecution in all parts of its range, and its total extinction is now only a matter of years."

Three years after this dismal prophecy was published, several trumpeters were seen in Yellowstone Park, and in 1919 two mated pairs were reported living in the Park, but nothing was done immediately to encourage them. In 1922 a biologist from the Biological Survey (now the Bureau of Sport Fisheries and Wildlife) visited Red Rock Lakes and recognized the desirability of buying the area as a refuge for the diminishing number of trumpeters that lived there.

Finally, in 1929, the National Park Service began a series of scientific studies of animals and birds in the parks, including the trumpeters in Yellowstone. The trumpeter survey was far from encouraging. It noted heavy egg loss and a very high mortality among the cygnets from predators and other adverse conditions. Moreover, once frightened by anything such as gunfire —even though the shooting was at ducks and not at them—the trumpeters remained suspicious and flighty for three or four years.

Concern mounted among the conservationists, and a team was appointed especially to study the trumpeters and do what it could to save them. It consisted of George Wright and Ben Thompson, Park Service biologists, and Dr. Joseph Dixon of the University of California. They were strongly supported by Roger Toll, Yellowstone superintendent.

About this same time, ranchers in the Red Rock Lakes country reported to Park authorities that swans as well as ducks were being shot. Wright wrote many letters to duck-hunting clubs, explaining the plight of the swans. The Montana Fish and Game Department was persuaded to post a reward payable to anyone who furnished information about swan shooters. In 1931, Dr. Dixon published an effective article about the plight of the trumpeters in *American Forests,* and for the first time the public was aroused.

Meantime the authorities in Yellowstone Park set up a predator control system to reduce the population of

By the early 20th century, once teeming populations of trumpeter swans (left) had dwindled to fewer than 100 in the United States. Since then, efforts such as establishing Red Rock Lakes National Wildlife Refuge and studying the bird's behavior and breeding habits there and at zoos (above) have helped them increase their population to 878 in 1978.

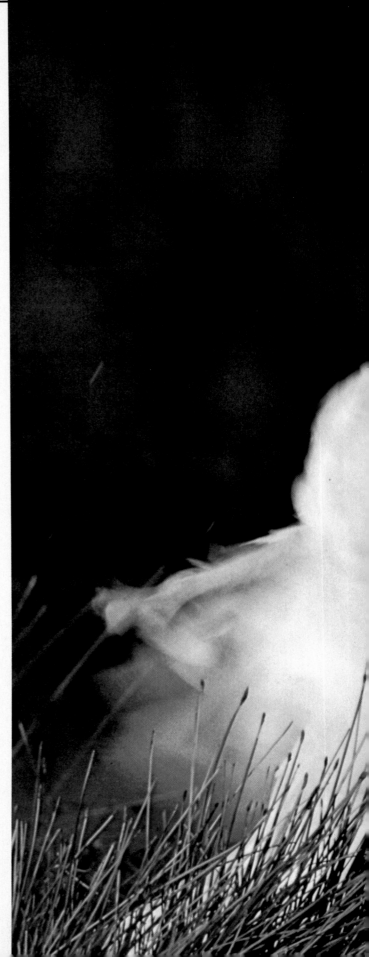

coyotes and ravens and give the baby swans a chance. Some of the Park's fishing waters near the trumpeters' nests were closed to the public, and Superintendent Toll relocated a main road then under construction to provide a buffer zone between the nesting swans and Park visitors.

But it was J. N. (Ding) Darling, famous cartoonist, militant conservationist, and first president of the National Wildlife Federation, who really saved the swans. For many years, through cartoons and eloquent speeches, he had publicized the cause of wildlife conservation and tirelessly flagellated the despoilers. In 1934 he was appointed Chief of the Biological Survey, and soon thereafter he visited Red Rock Lakes and promptly insisted that a refuge must be established there for the trumpeters. The Red Rock Lakes Refuge finally became a reality in 1935.

Even so, it seemed that the swans' troubles were not entirely ended. The Army now decided to set up a mountain training and artillery center near Henry's Lake in Idaho, where the trumpeters often appeared. Biologists knew from their studies that the roar of artillery would frighten the birds and make them wary of the whole mountain area where they lived. With the support of powerful conservationist groups, Refuge and Park authorities persuaded the Army to take its noisy training ground elsewhere.

It was also found that some trumpeters were still being shot illegally outside the Refuge, particularly in Idaho. A group called the Emergency Conservation Committee, headed by Rosalie Edge of New York, raised enough money to hire a lecturer, who spent two years in the mountain country stirring up the local citizens and persuading them to leave the swans alone. The lectures were heard by more than 24,000 people and were so effective that at last the shooting virtually ended.

At the time the Red Rock Lakes Refuge was established, in 1935, the Biological Survey reported that 46 of the 73 trumpeters left in this country made their home at Red Rock. Rigorous protection turned the tide, and slowly the great birds began to multiply. In 1966 aerial surveys counted 878 wild trumpeters in the contiguous United States, 417 of them in Montana. It is believed that there are also about a thousand in Western Canada and Alaska, and 84 live in captivity in the United States.

Thus the trumpeter swan is one of the very few threatened species in this country to be re-established in a substantial way.

Robert Murphy

**Library of Congress
Cataloging in Publication Data**

Main entry under title:

The Gift of birds.

Includes index.
  1. Birds.   I. National
Wildlife Federation.
QL676.G34   598.2   79-88427
ISBN O-912186-33-X

Text and Picture Credits

Text Credits

OF HOLLOW BONES AND TREETOP HOMES

  "The Nature of Birds" (p. 8), abridged from pp. 67-8, 90-3, 94-6 "The Nature of Birds" in *The Adventure of Birds* by Charlton Ogburn. Copyright © 1975 by Charlton Ogburn. By permission of William Morrow & Company.

  "Of Feather and Wing" (p. 14), from *Song of the Sky* by Guy Murchie. Reprinted by permission of the author.

  "The Mysterious Magic of Birdsong" (p. 18), reprinted with permission from the May 1962 *Reader's Digest.* Copyright ©1962 by The Reader's Digest Assn., Inc.

  "How Red the Tooth and Claw?" (p. 20), from *Wild Heritage* by Sally Carrighar. Copyright © by Sally Carrighar. Reprinted by permission of Houghton Mifflin Company.

  "A Couple of Pebbles . . . A Ton of Twigs" (p. 28), copyright 1975 by the National Wildlife Federation. Reprinted from the May/June issue of *International Wildlife* Magazine.

  "Growing Wings" (p. 30), from *Growing Wings* by Sarita Van Vleck, William L. Bauhan Publisher, 1975.

  "Vanity Has Nothing to Do with Preening" (p. 32), copyright 1978 by the National Wildlife Federation. Reprinted from the July/August issue of *International Wildlife* Magazine.

  "The Wonders of Bird Navigation" (p. 34), from *Horticulture* Magazine, November 1974. Reprinted by permission of Gordon M. Snyder.

TAKING A CLOSER LOOK

  "The Hunters of the Moonlight" (p. 38), reprinted by permission of Dodd, Mead & Company, Inc. from *Dwellers of the Silences* by Alexander Sprunt, Jr. Copyright 1931, 1959 by Alexander Sprunt, Jr.

  "Protecting the Nest" (p. 42), from *The Book of Owls* by Lewis Wayne Walker. Copyright © 1974 by Melanie Walker Rankin. Condensed by permission of Alfred A. Knopf, Inc.

  "Nature's Little Dynamos" (p. 46), from *Hummingbirds* by Crawford H. Greenewalt, American Museum of Natural History, 1960.

  "One Day at Teton Marsh" (p. 48), from *One Day at Teton Marsh* by Sally Carrighar. Copyright © 1947 by the Curtis Publishing Co. Copyright © 1945, 1946, 1947 and renewed 1975 by Sally Carrighar. Condensed by permission of Alfred A. Knopf, Inc.

  "Listening Point" (p. 52), from *Listening Point* by Sigurd F. Olson. Copyright © 1958 by Sigurd F. Olson. Condensed by permission of Alfred A. Knopf, Inc.

  "The Gloomiest Bird" (p. 56), reprinted by permission from *Stories from Under the Sky* by John Madson © 1961 by The Iowa State University Press, Ames, Iowa.

  "Tundra Magic" (p. 60), excerpts from *Eskimo Year: A Naturalist's Adventure in the Far North* by George Miksch Sutton, published by Macmillan Publishing Co., Inc., 1934.

  "Flood Tide" (p. 62), from *Under the Sea-Wind* by Rachel L. Carson. Copyright 1941 by Rachel L. Carson, renewed 1969 by Roger Christie. Reprinted by permission of Oxford University Press, Inc.

IN THE SERVICE OF MAN

  "Chickens, Chickens, Chickens" (p. 68), reprinted by permission of the publisher, Elsevier/Nelson Books from *Chickens, Chickens, Chickens* by Peter R. Limburg. Copyright © 1975 by Peter R. Limburg.

  "Hung, Strung, and Potted" (p. 72), taken from *Hung, Strung, and Potted* by Sally Smith Booth. Copyright © 1971 by Sally Smith Booth. Used by permission of Clarkson N. Potter, Inc.

  "Grouse Feathers" (p. 74), taken from *Grouse Feathers* by Burton L. Spiller. Copyright © 1972 by Burton L. Spiller. Used by permission of Crown Publishers, Inc.

  "Fishing with Feathered Lightning" (p. 78), copyright 1971 by the National Wildlife Federation. Reprinted from the July/August issue of *International Wildlife* Magazine.

  "The Goshawk" (p. 80), condensation of Chapter 1 from *The Goshawk* by T. H. White, published by Jonathan Cape Ltd. and G. P. Putnam's Sons, 1951.

  Quote by Richard K. Mathews (p. 85), excerpt from *Wild Animals as Pets* by Richard K. Mathews. Copyright © 1971 by Richard K. Mathews. Reprinted by permission of Doubleday & Company, Inc.

"Never Underestimate the Power of a Pigeon" (p. 86), copyright 1973 by the National Wildlife Federation. Reprinted from the September/October issue of *International Wildlife* Magazine.

"The Useful Goose" (p. 88), reprinted by permission of Jack Denton Scott.

FLIGHTS OF INSPIRATION

"The American Eagle" (p. 102), reprinted from *The Folk Arts and Crafts of New England* by Priscilla Sawyer Lord and Daniel J. Foley. Copyright © 1965, 1975 by the authors. Reprinted with the permission of the publisher, Chilton Book Co., Radnor, PA.

"America's Native Wildlife Art Form" (p. 104), copyright 1967 by the National Wildlife Federation. Reprinted from the October/November issue of *National Wildlife* Magazine.

"Seagulls" (p. 109), copyright © 1943, 1971 by Robert Francis. Reprinted by permission from *Robert Francis: The Collected Poems, 1943-1976* (University of Massachusetts Press, 1976).

"Pigeons" (p. 109), from *Differences* by Richard Kell. Used by permission of the publisher, Chatto and Windus, Ltd.

"A Bird Came Down the Walk" (p. 109), reprinted by permission of the publisher from *The Poems of Emily Dickinson,* edited by Thomas H. Johnson, Cambridge, Mass.: The Belknap Press of Harvard University Press. Copyright © 1951, 1955 by the President and Fellows of Harvard College.

"Twilight Whippoorwill . . ." (p. 109), by Basho, from *Japanese Haiku,* copyright © 1955-1956, Peter Pauper Press.

"Something Told the Wild Geese" (p. 109), reprinted with permission of Macmillan Publishing Co., Inc. from *Branches Green* by Rachel Field. Copyright 1934 by Macmillan Publishing Co., Inc., renewed 1962 by Arthur S. Pederson.

"The Darkling Thrush" (p. 109), from *Collected Poems of Thomas Hardy,* Macmillan Publishing Co., Inc., 1953.

"The Birds of America" (p. 110), from *A Long Undressing, Collected Poems 1949-1969* by James Broughton, published by The Jargon Society.

"Ducks' Ditty" (p. 110), from *The Wind in the Willows* by Kenneth Grahame is used by permission of Charles Scribner's Sons. Copyright 1908 Charles Scribner's Sons.

"The Ptarmigan" (p. 110), reprinted with permission of William Collins Publishers, Inc. from *The Birds and the Beasts Were There* by William Cole. Copyright © 1963 by William Cole.

"Fable of the Talented Mockingbird" (p. 110), from *The Carleton Miscellany,* copyright © 1961 by Carleton College.

"The Wild Swans at Coole" (p. 110), reprinted with permission of Macmillan Publishing Co., Inc. from *The Collected Poems of William Butler Yeats* by William Butler Yeats. Copyright 1919 by Macmillan Publishing Co., Inc., renewed 1947 by Bertha Georgie Yeats.

"The Bird of Night" (p. 110), reprinted with permission of Macmillan Publishing Co., Inc. from *The Bat-Poet* by Randall Jarrell. Copyright Macmillan Publishing Co., Inc., 1963, 1964.

"November Sunrise . . ." (p. 110), by Kakei, from *Japanese Haiku,* copyright © 1955-56, Peter Pauper Press.

BIRD WATCHERS ON BIRD WATCHING

"The Moment of Discovery . . . A Lifetime of Rewards," selection by John James Audubon (p. 123), from *Audubon, by Himself,* edited by Alice Ford, published by Doubleday & Company, Inc. Selections by Julian Huxley (pp. 123, 126), from *Bird-Watching and Bird Behaviour* by Julian Huxley, reprinted by permission of A D Peters & Co. Ltd. Selection by Louis J. Halle (p. 126), from pp. 69-70, 72 in *Spring in Washington,* decennial edition by Louis J. Halle, Jr. Copyright 1947, 1957 by Louis J. Halle, Jr., Harper & Row. Selection by Theodore Roosevelt (p. 127), from *Theodore Roosevelt's America,* Farida A. Wiley, Editor. Reprinted by permission of The Devin-Adair Co., Old Greenwich, CT. Copyright © 1955 by The Devin-Adair Company.

"Birds Among the Skyscrapers" (p. 130), reprinted by permission of Dodd, Mead & Company, Inc. from *Birds Over America* by Roger Tory Peterson. Copyright © 1948, 1964, 1976 by Roger Tory Peterson.

"On the Wings of a Bird" (p. 137), from *On the Wings of a Bird,* by Herbert Ravenel Sass, published by Doubleday & Company, Inc.

"Have You Started Your Life List?" (p. 140), reprinted with permission

from the June 1975 *Reader's Digest.* Copyright © 1975 by The Reader's Digest Assn., Inc.

"Up from the Egg: The Confessions of a Nuthatch Avoider" (p. 142), from *Verses from 1929 On* by Ogden Nash, by permission of Little, Brown and Co. Copyright © 1956 by Ogden Nash.

SHARING A SHRINKING PLANET

"Glimpsing the Darkness" (p. 146), selection by Theodore Roosevelt, used by permission of Charles Scribner's Sons from *A Book Lover's Holidays in the Open* by Theodore Roosevelt. Copyright 1916 Charles Scribner's Sons; renewal copyright 1944 by Edith K. Carow. Selection by Henry Beetle Hough, reprinted with permission of the *Vineyard Gazette.*

"The Last Parakeet" (p. 148), a condensation of "The Last Parakeet" by George Laycock which appeared in *Audubon.* Copyright © 1969 The National Audubon Society. Used by permission.

"Men, Birds, and Adventure" (p. 150), from *Men, Birds, and Adventure* by Virginia Eifert. Used by permission of Lawrence Eifert.

"Take a Long, Last Look at the Condor" (p. 154), copyright 1974 by the National Wildlife Federation. Reprinted from the April/May issue of *National Wildlife* Magazine.

"The View from Hawk Mountain " (p. 156), condensed from pp. 13-25 of *The View from Hawk Mountain* by Michael Harwood with the permission of Charles Scribner's Sons. Copyright © 1973 Michael Harwood.

"Egrets and the Plume Trade" (p. 160), from pp. 86-89 of *Lost Wild America* by Robert M. McClung. Copyright © 1969 by Robert M. McClung. By permission of William Morrow & Company.

"Adventures in Bird Protection" (p. 162), reprinted by permission of Hawthorn Books, Inc. from *Adventures in Bird Protection* by Thomas Gilbert Pearson. Originally published by Appleton-Century Co., 1937. All rights reserved.

"Triumph of the Trumpeters" (p. 166), copyright 1967 by the National Wildlife Federation. Reprinted from the June/July issue of *National Wildlife* Magazine.

Picture Credits

Cover: Young mockingbird, Laura Riley/Bruce Coleman, Inc. Page 1: Pine siskin, Jen and Des Bartlett/Bruce Coleman, Inc. 2-3: Ducks and geese at Klamath, Oregon, ANIMALS ANIMALS/© Margot Conte.

OF HOLLOW BONES AND TREETOP HOMES

Pages 6-7: Prairie falcon in flight, Ron Austing. 8: Flamingo, Tom Stack/ TOM STACK & ASSOCIATES. Red-bellied woodpecker, William J. Weber. Kestrel, G. C. Kelley. Evening grosbeak, William Tompkin. Least bittern, Jack Dermid. 9: Yellow-breasted chat, John L. Tveten. 10: Bluebird, Ron Austing/ Bruce Coleman, Inc. 11: Gull feather, David Cavagnaro. 12: Hollow bone, Robert L. Dunne. 13: Gull's skeleton, Andreas Feininger/Life Magazine, © 1951, Time Inc. 14: Bird landing, Jodi Cobb/Woodfin Camp, Inc. 14-15: Duck flight sequence, Ad Cameron, from *Birds: Their Life, Their Ways, Their World,* illustrations by Ad Cameron, text by Dr. Christopher Perrins. Copyright © 1976 in Switzerland by Elsevier Publishing Projects, S. A., Lausanne. Published in 1976 by Harry N. Abrams, Inc., New York. 16: Albatross, Jonathan Blair/Woodfin Camp, Inc. 16-17: Pelican landing, M. P. Kahl. Pelicans on a river, M. P. Kahl. 17: Swan flight sequence, Wayne Scherr/ TOM STACK & ASSOCIATES. 19: Red-winged blackbird, C. Gable Ray. 20: Whooping crane, Ron Dillow/TOM STACK & ASSOCIATES. 20-21: Flamingos, Clem Haagner/Bruce Coleman, Inc. 22: Sage grouse: top, K. W. Fink/Bruce Coleman, Inc.; middle, Leonard Lee Rue III/Bruce Coleman, Inc.; bottom, Joseph Van Wormer/Bruce Coleman, Inc. 22-23: Canada geese, Joy Spurr/Bruce Coleman, Inc. 24-25: Frigate birds, Jen and Des Bartlett/Bruce Coleman, Inc. 25: Ruffed grouse drumming sequence, Harvey Hansen. 26: Bluebirds, Thase Daniel. Wild turkeys, Leonard Lee Rue III/FPG. Goldfinches, Thase Daniel/Bruce Coleman, Inc. 27: Cape gannets, Gerald Cubitt. 28: Eagle's nest, James L. Leard. Adelie penguin on nest, Roger Tory Peterson. 29: Guanay and king cormorants nesting, Jen and Des Bartlett/Bruce Coleman, Inc. Chimney swift nest, Hal H. Harrison. Cliff swallows' nests, Grant Heilman. Short-billed marsh wren nest, Hal H. Harrison. Social weaver nest, K. W.

Fink/Bruce Coleman, Inc. 30: Wood thrush, William D. Griffin. Field sparrows, Ron Austing. 31: Wood duck hatching sequence: left, top right and middle right, William J. Weber; bottom right, Thase Daniel. 32: Anhinga, Robert C. Gildart. 33: Duck preening sequence, Joseph Van Wormer. 35: Migrating Canada geese, Grant Heilman.

TAKING A CLOSER LOOK

Pages 36-37: Swans, Teiji Saga/Pacific Press. 38: Big Cypress Swamp, James H. Carmichael, Jr. 40: Great blue heron in flight, C. Allan Morgan. 40-41: Great blue heron feeding, Tom Myers. 41: Great blue heron with young, Robert Pelham. 42: Long-eared owl: top left and right, Ron Austing; bottom, ANIMALS ANIMALS/© Zig Leszczynski. 43: Long-eared owl, ANIMALS ANIMALS/© Zig Leszczynski. 45: Blue jay, Dan McPeek. 46: Blue-throated hummingbird, Lois Cox. 46-47: Long-tailed sylph hummingbird, Karl Weidmann. Calliope hummingbird, David H. Carriere. 48: Grand Teton National Park, Russell Lamb. 49: Osprey in flight, Laura Riley/Bruce Coleman, Inc. 51: Young osprey, Jack Dermid. 53: Canoe on lake, Les Blacklock. 54: Loon on shore, Kip Taylor. 55: Loon painting by Owen J. Gromme, courtesy of Mr. and Mrs. Dan Greenwood and Owen J. Gromme. 56: Turkey vulture closeup, Robert L. Dunne. Turkey vulture in flight, Norman Owen Tomalin/Bruce Coleman, Inc. Turkey vultures in tree, M. P. L. Fogden/Bruce Coleman, Inc. 57: Turkey vultures on cactus, Jen and Des Bartlett/Bruce Coleman, Inc. 58: Water ouzel: top, Ed Cesar; middle, Jeff Foott/Bruce Coleman, Inc.; bottom, ANIMALS ANIMALS/© Stouffer Enterprises. Yosemite waterfall, Tom Myers. 60-61: Rock ptarmigan, Edgar T. Jones/ Bruce Coleman, Inc. 61: Baffin Island, Francisco Erize/Bruce Coleman, Inc. 62-63: Skimmers in tandem, Larry R. Ditto/Bruce Coleman, Inc. 63: Skimmers shading eggs, ANIMALS ANIMALS/© Fred E. Unverhau. Skimmer with chicks, ANIMALS ANIMALS/© William D. Griffin. 65: Hedge sparrow and cuckoo, John Markham/Bruce Coleman, Inc.

IN THE SERVICE OF MAN

Pages 66-67: Rooster and hens, Hans Reinhard/Bruce Coleman, Inc. 68: Red jungle fowl, Joseph Van Wormer/Bruce Coleman, Inc. 70: Egg production line, John Colwell/Grant Heilman. 71: Long-tailed fowl, E. Miyazawa/Black Star. 72: Colonial kitchen, John Lewis Stage/The Image Bank. 74-75: "Hunting the Edges" by Robert Abbett, Sportsman's Edge, Ltd., N.Y.C. 77: Ruffed grouse, Gregory Scott/National Audubon Society Collection/P. R. 78: "Cormorant" by Miyamoto Niten, Jean Dominique LAJOUX. 78-79: "Cormorant Fishing on the Nagara River" by Keisai Eisen, courtesy of the Fogg Art Museum, Harvard University, Duel Collection. 81: Goshawk, ANIMALS ANIMALS/© Bruce Macdonald. 82: Falconer, Eric Hosking/Bruce Coleman, Inc. 84: Ostrich race, C. J. Hadley. Cockfight, Kay Chernush/ The Image Bank. 84-85: Macaws, Jen and Des Bartlett/Bruce Coleman, Inc. 85: Canaries, Hans Reinhard/Bruce Coleman, Inc. Pigeon raiser and pigeon "war," Alfred Eisenstaedt/Life Magazine, © 1978, Time Inc. 86: Soldier with pigeon, U. S. Army. Lab technician, Wide World Photos. 87: Pigeon race, Martin Rogers/Woodfin Camp, Inc. Pigeon buyers, Martin Rogers/Woodfin Camp, Inc. 89: Goose, Tom Myers. 90: Hissing goose, Lynn M. Stone. Geese guarding distillery, exterior and interior, courtesy of George Ballantine & Son, Ltd. 91: Weeder geese, Willma Gore.

FLIGHTS OF INSPIRATION

Pages 92-93: "Evening Mood" by Manfred Schatz, courtesy of Russell A. Fink. 94: Wilson's "Ruffed Grouse," Albert Kilbertus. Catesby's "Passenger Pigeon," James P. Valentine (Quest Foundation). 95: Audubon's "Osprey with Trout," courtesy of the New-York Historical Society. 96: Audubon's "Green Herons and Luna Moth," courtesy of *The Living World of Audubon* by Roland C. Clement, a Ridge Press Book. 97: Fuertes's "Gyrfalcon," Laboratory of Ornithology, Cornell University. Fuertes's "Eastern Kingbird," U. S. Fish & Wildlife Service. Jaques's "Chinese Golden Pheasant," courtesy of Glenbow Museum, Calgary, Alberta. 98: Peterson's "Snowy Owls," courtesy of the artist and Mill Pond Press, Inc., Venice, Florida. 99: Eckelberry's "Spruce Grouse," courtesy of Frame House Gallery. Sutton's "Sutton's Warbler," courtesy of Frame House Gallery. Reece's "Pheasant Country," courtesy of the artist and Mill Pond Press, Inc., Venice, Florida. 100: Ripper's "Great Horned Owl," courtesy of Chuck Ripper. Lansdowne's "Golden-winged Warbler," M. F. Feheley Arts Co., Ltd. 100-101: Ede's "Mallard," courtesy of Newman Galleries, Inc. 102:

Tavern sign, courtesy of The Connecticut Historical Society. 103: Eagle from Lincoln's barge, courtesy of United States Naval Academy Museum. Eagle carver, Michael Philip Manheim/Photo Researchers, Inc. 105: Indian reed decoy, The Museum of the American Indian, Heye Foundation. Preening Canada goose decoy, M. E. Warren Photography. Decoy art, Arthur J. Anderson. 106: Edwards's "Dodo," Leighton Warren, courtesy of Blacker-Wood Library, McGill University. 108: Sooty terns, Jonathan Blair/Woodfin Camp, Inc. 111: Bluebirds, Michael L. Smith. 112: Roc, from *The Book of the Thousand Nights and a Night* by Richard Burton (1885). 113: Phoenix, The Free Library of Philadelphia. 114: Caladrius, New York Public Library. 115: Basilisk, from *A Fantastic Bestiary* by Ernst and Johanna Lehner. 116: Migrating geese, William D. Griffin. 117: White wagtails, Hans Reinhard/ Bruce Coleman, Inc. English robin, Hans Reinhard/Bruce Coleman, Inc. Crows, Dan Sudia/National Audubon Society Collection/P. R. Sarus crane, George H. Harrison. 118: Barn swallows, Stephen Dalton /NHPA. 119: Bird of Paradise, Constance P. Warner.

BIRD WATCHERS ON BIRD WATCHING

Pages 120-121: Child with bird, David Caccia. 122: Vermont country road, Richard W. Brown. 124: Catbird, Marilyn Krog. Western meadowlark, Anthony Mercieca/National Audubon Society Collection/P.R. Gilded flicker, Jen and Des Bartlett/Bruce Coleman, Inc. Cedar waxwing, Gilbert Staender. Chickadee, George H. Harrison. Robin, Ron Austing. 125: Wood thrush, Hal H. Harrison. Myrtle warbler, Larry Ditto/Bruce Coleman, Inc. Green woodpecker, Hans Reinhard/Bruce Coleman, Inc. Tufted titmouse, William D. Griffin/Shostal Associates. Chipping sparrow, L. West. Yellow warbler, Don Wollander. 126: Eastern meadowlark, Harold Hoffman/ National Audubon Society Collection/P.R. Black-throated blue warbler, Ron Austing/Bruce Coleman, Inc. 127: American bittern, William D. Griffin. 128-129: Mallards and pintail ducks, Thomas D. Mangelsen. 130: Central Park, Peter B. Kaplan/Photo Researchers, Inc. 132: Starlings, A. J. Deane/ Bruce Coleman, Inc. 133: Purple martin house, Rod Cochran. House sparrow, Sidney Bahrt. Gull on table, J. Kraay/Bruce Coleman, Inc. Robin in traffic light, Nathan Zabarsky. 134: Scarlet tanager, Leonard Lee Rue III. 135: Purple gallinule, Thase Daniel. 136: Sass home and garden, Tom Blagden, Jr. 138: The Sass garden, Tom Blagden, Jr. 139: Prothonotary warblers, Eldred Montgomery. Parula warblers, Thase Daniel. Hooded warbler, Dan Sudia/National Audubon Society Collection/P.R. Black-and-white warbler, James H. Carmichael, Jr./Bruce Coleman, Inc. White-throated sparrow, Leonard Lee Rue III. Prairie warbler, Thase Daniel. Yellow-crowned night heron, ANIMALS ANIMALS/© C. C. Lockwood. Cardinal, Grant Heilman. Red-breasted nuthatch, Stephen J. Krasemann/Daniel Krasemann. Pine siskin, Kevin Byron/Bruce Coleman, Inc. 140: California gull, R. L. Kothenbeutel. 143: Superb starling, George H. Harrison.

SHARING A SHRINKING PLANET

Pages 144-145: Birds on the wing, ENTHEOS. 146: Theodore Roosevelt on beach, Theodore Roosevelt Collection, Harvard College Library. 147: Heath hen, Dr. Alfred O. Gross from Wildlife Management Institute. Martha's Vineyard, Alfred Eisenstaedt/Life Magazine, © 1961, Time Inc. 149: "Carolina Paraquets," John A. Ruthven. 150: Ornithologist in swamp, Bird Photographs, Inc. 151: Catesby's "Ivory-billed Woodpecker," James P. Valentine (Quest Foundation). 152: Ivory-billed woodpeckers nesting and James Tanner with parabolic microphone, Bird Photographs, Inc. 153: Dr. Arthur Allen, Bird Photographs, Inc. 155: California condor, Dave Siddon. 157: Dead hawks, Richard Pough, courtesy of Hawk Mountain Sanctuary. 158: Red-tailed hawk, Thase Daniel. 158-159: Observers on Hawk Mountain, Ron Austing. 160: Snowy egret, R. Kawahami/The Image Bank. 161: Woman in plumed hat, National Audubon Society. 162: Political placard from *Adventures in Bird Protection* by Thomas Gilbert Pearson. Originally published by Appleton-Century Company, Inc., 1937, courtesy Hawthorn Books, Inc. 163: Black-crowned night herons, ENTHEOS. 164: Malheur refuge drying up, Oregon Historical Society. Wilson's phalarope, Rachel Lamoreux. 164-165: Cranes and geese, ENTHEOS. 165: Horned grebe, Harry Engels. Yellow-headed blackbird, ENTHEOS. Double-crested cormorants, David Hatler. 166-167: Trumpeter swan with cygnet, Harry Engels. 167: Trumpeter swan family, Philadelphia Zoological Garden. 168-169: Trumpeter swan, Robert B. Smith.

National Wildlife Federation

1412 16th St., N. W.
Washington, D. C. 20036

Thomas L. Kimball,
Executive Vice President

J. A. Brownridge,
Administrative Vice President

James D. Davis,
Director, Book Development

Staff for this Book

Howard F. Robinson,
Editor

Constance Brown Boltz,
Art Director

Victor H. Waldrop,
Art Editor

Jane Johnston Dutton,
Research Editor

Mel Baughman,
Production Manager

Cathy Pelletier,
Permissions Editor

Robyn Gregg,
Editorial Assistant

Tina Bandle,
Production Artist

Patricia L. Matsos,
Production Artist

Acknowledgments

For help in locating art, photographs, and special information from far-flung parts of the United States, we are indebted to many people who have given generously of their time and expertise, including Mr. Wallace Finley Dailey, Curator, Theodore Roosevelt Collection, Harvard College Library; Mr. Larry R. Ditto, Assistant Refuge Manager, Malheur National Wildlife Refuge; Mr. Paul E. Ewing, III, Assistant Photographs Librarian, Oregon Historical Society; Ms. Genevieve Prlain, Registrar, The Oakland Museum, Oakland, California; Mr. Thompson R. Harlow, Director, The Connecticut Historical Society; and the reference librarians at the Library of Congress and the Fairfax (Virginia) Public Library.

We also owe thanks to the following people at NWF who have made our task easier: Jenafred Shore, Librarian; the staff of the Raptor Information Center; Craig Tufts and Susan Ennett, Naturalists; and the editors of *National Wildlife* and *International Wildlife* magazines and of *Ranger Rick's Nature Magazine.*